COSTING

COSTING
An introduction

TEACHER'S MANUAL

FOURTH EDITION

Colin Drury

Professor, Department of Accountancy and Finance,
University of Huddersfield
UK

INTERNATIONAL THOMSON BUSINESS PRESS
I ⓉP® An International Thomson Publishing Company

London • Bonn • Johannesburg • Madrid • Melbourne • Mexico City • New York • Paris
Singapore • Tokyo • Toronto • Albany, NY • Belmont, CA • Cincinnati, OH • Detroit, MI

Costing: An Introduction (Teacher's Manual)

Copyright © 1987, 1990, 1994 and 1999 Colin Drury

I(T)P®   A division of International Thomson Publishing Inc.
The ITP log is a trademark under licence

British Library Cataloguing-in-Publication Data
A catalogue record for this book is available from the British Library

First edition 1987
Second edition 1990
Third edition 1994 (all published by Chapman & Hall)

Fourth edition 1999 by International Thomson Business Press

Typeset by Columns Design Ltd, Reading, Berkshire
Printed in the UK by The Alden Press, Osney Mead, Oxford

ISBN 1-86152-277-0

International Thomson Business Press
Berkshire House
168–173 High Holborn
London WC1V 7AA
UK

http://www.itbp.com

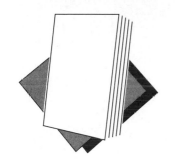

Contents

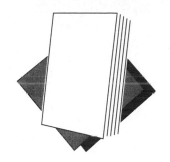

Preface

This manual is complementary to the main book *Costing: An introduction* and to the corresponding *Students' Manual.* The aim of the main text is to focus on an understanding of the principles and practice of cost and management accounting whereas the aim of the accompanying manuals is to focus on the application of the principles to a wide range of problems.

It is essential that the student works through such a range of problems to gain experience in the application of principles but generally there is insufficient classroom time for tutorial guidance. The *Students' Manual* provides this guidance by enabling the student to work independently on problems and referring to the suggested solutions.

The *Teachers' Manual* provides solutions which are not generally available to students. The objective is to provide tutors with feedback information on the students' ability to solve problems independently. A short description of each problem is given at the beginning of each chapter to enable tutors to select problems which are appropriate to specific courses.

Finally I would like to thank, once again, the Institute of Chartered Accountants in England and Wales, the Chartered Association of Certified Accountants, the Chartered Institute of Cost and Management Accountants, the Association of Accounting Technicians, the Joint Matriculation Board and the Associated Examining board for permission to reproduce problems which have appeared in past examinations. The answers to the problems are my own and are in no way the approved solutions of the above professional bodies.

Cost and revenue classification

Answers to Chapter 2

Question summary

2.1 to 2.5
Multiple choice questions.

2.6 to 2.12
Essay questions on cost classification. Note that Question 2.9 also includes a discussion of the role of the cost accountant. The answers to some of these questions are contained within the chapter and therefore the answers consist of a reference to the appropriate section in Chapter 2.

2.13
A multiple choice style question relating to cost behaviour.

2.14
An essay question requiring a description of different cost terms.

2.15 to 2.17
Short questions which can be used to test your understandine of cost classification.

2.18
A description of various cost terms – discretionary, variable, fixed, notional and opportunity costs. The question also requires the student to indicate whether a project should be continued or abandoned based on a comparison of relevant revenues with relevant costs.

2.19
A more demanding and time-consuming Foundation/Stage 1 question relating to cost behaviour.

2.20
Calculation of a product cost and extraction of relevant costs for decision-making.

2.21
Calculation of a product cost for cost-plus pricing.

2.22
Computation and discussion of relevant, sunk and opportunity costs for decision-making.

2.23
Ascertaining the relevant cost of car journeys and the estimation of costs at 80% of budgeted activity.

Answer to question 2.16

(1) (a); (2) (d); (3) (e); (4) (f); (5) (i); (6) (b); (7) (h).

Answer to question 2.17

(i) Direct materials: 9
(ii) Direct labour: 16
(iii) Direct expenses: 10
(iv) Indirect production overhead: 1, 6, 8, 18, 19
(v) Research and development costs: 20
(vi) Selling and distribution costs: 7, 11, 12, 13, 17
(vii) Administration costs: 2, 3, 4, 14, 15
(viii) Finance costs: 5

Answer to question 2.20

(a) Variable cost per running hour of Machine XR1

		£
	(£27,500/1,100 hours) =	25
Fixed cost ,, ,, ,, ,, ,, ,,	(£20,000/1,100 hours) =	18.182

Cost of a brain scan on Machine XRI:	£
Variable machine cost (4 hrs × £25)	100
X-ray plates	40
Total variable cost	140
Fixed machine cost (4 hours × £18.182)	72.73
Total cost of a scan	212.73
Total cost of a satisfactory scan (£212.73/0.9)	236.37

(b) It is assumed that fixed costs will remain unchanged and also that they are not relevant to the decision. The relevant costs are the incremental costs of an additional scan:

Machine XR1:	£
Variable cost per scan	140
Variable cost per satisfactory scan (£140/0.9)	155.56

Machine XR50:	
Variable machine cost per scan (£64,000/2,000 hrs × 1.8 hours)	57.60
X-ray plates	55.00
Variable cost per scan	112.60
Variable cost per satisfactory scan (£112.60/0.94)	119.79

The relevant costs per satisfactory scan are cheaper on Machine XR50 and therefore brain scans should be undertaken on this machine.

Answer to question 2.21

(a) *Standard* cost *sheet (per unit):*

	(£)	(£)
Direct materials 40 m² at £5.30 per m²		212
Direct wages:		
Bonding dept 48 hours at £2.50 per hour	120	
Finishing dept 30 hours at £1.90 per hour	57	
		177
(i) Prime cost		389
Variable overhead:ᵃ		
Bonding dept 48 hours at £0.75 per hour	36	
Finishing dept 30 hours at £0.50 per hour	15	
		51
(ii) Variable production cost		440
Fixed production overheadᵇ		40
(iii) Total production cost		480
Selling and distribution costᶜ	20	
Administration costᶜ	10	
		30
(iv) Total cost		510

Notes:

ᵃ Variable overhead rates: $\text{Bonding} = \dfrac{£375,000}{500,000 \text{ hours}} = £0.75$

$\text{Finishing} = \dfrac{£150,000}{300,000 \text{ hours}} = £0.50$

ᵇ Fixed production overhead rate per unit of output $= \dfrac{£392,000}{9,800 \text{ units}} = £40$

The fixed production overhead rate per unit of output has been calculated because there appears to be only one product produced. Alternatively, a fixed production hourly overhead rate can be calculated and charged to the product on the basis of the number of hours which the product spends in each department.

^{c} Selling and production cost per unit of output $= \dfrac{£196,000}{9,800 \text{ units}} = £20$

Administration cost per unit of output $= \dfrac{£98,000}{9,800 \text{ units}} = £10$

(b)   Selling price per unit $£510 \times \dfrac{100}{85} = \underline{\underline{£600}}$

Accounting for materials and labour

Answers to Chapter 3

Question summary

3.1
Multiple choice question.

3.2 to 3.8
Various essay questions on topics related to Chapter 3.

3.9 to 3.12
Computations for various stores pricing methods. Questions 3.10 and 3.12 also require the calculation of EOQ. In addition, the final part of Question 3.12 requires the computation of maximum and minimum stock levels and the reorder point.

3.13
This question consists of two parts: stores pricing and labour cost accounting.

3.14
A simple question which is useful for illustrating some of the issues to be considered when introducing an incentive scheme.

3.15 to 3.17
Calculation of earnings based on hourly rates, piecework and bonus schemes.

3.18
Accounting treatment of holiday pay and overtime plus a computation and evaluation of a time rate and incentive payment system.

3.19
Calculation of labour turnover percentage and efficiency ratio and a discussion of how labour turnover can be reduced.

3.20 and 3.21
These are more difficult problems which focus on the effects of introducing incentive schemes.

Answer to question 3.2

For the answer to this question see the sections on materials control procedure and treatment of stores losses in Chapter 3. In particular the answer should stress the need for a system of perpetual inventory – that is, a system which involves the recording of each stock movement on a bin card or computerized record so that the balance of every item in stock is always available. The answer should also include discussion of:

(i) the importance of setting target stock levels and order quantities for each stock item and of regularly comparing actual stocks against target;

(ii) ordering procedure;

(iii) receiving procedure;

(iv) issue procedure;

(v) comparison of actual stock with clerical records by means of complete periodic stock count or some form of continuous stocktaking.

Answer to question 3.4

See Chapter 3 for the answer to this question.

Answer to question 3.7

(a) The information and procedures required are:

(i) Each batch should be given a separate batch identifying number, and all costs should be attached to this number.

(ii) A system of material issue requisitions should be in use, and the appropriate batch number can be entered on the requisitions.

(iii) The material issues should be priced from the stores ledger using a FIFO, LIFO or weighted average system.

For a more detailed explanation of the procedure see the sections on materials control procedure and pricing the issue of raw materials in Chapter 3.

(b) The elements included in an operative's gross wages are:

(i) basic wage;

(ii) overtime earnings;

(iii) shift premium; and

(iv) bonus.

For the basic wage earnings the hours directly attributable to the product multiplied by the hourly wage rate will be regarded as part of the prime cost. Any wages in respect of non-productive time which cannot be directly traced to the components is not part of prime cost, and should be charged to overheads. For an explanation of the remaining items see the section on accounting treatment of various labour cost items in Chapter 3.

Answer to question 3.8

(a)   See the section on idle time in Chaper 3 for the answer to this question.

(b)   There is no standard report form, but the drafted form should provide information on the number of hours of idle time and hours of idle time as a percentage of total hours for the current period. This information should also be presented on a cumulative basis. In addition the form should provide an analysis of idle time by causes – avoidable and unavoidable. Examples of avoidable causes are awaiting instructions, awaiting materials and awaiting repairs. Examples of unavoidable causes are machine breakdowns and power failure.

Answer to question 3.9

(a)   (i)   *Stores ledger card – FIFO method:*

Date	Receipts Qty	Price £	Value £	Issues Qty	Price £	Value £	Balance Qty	Value £
1 April							40	400
4 April	140	11	1,540				180	1,940
10 April				40	10	400		
				50	11	550		
				90		950	90	990
12 April	60	12	720				150	1,710
13 April				90	11	990		
				10	12	120		
				100		1,110	50	600
16 April	200	10	2,000				250	2,600
21 April				50	12	600		
				20	10	200	180	1,800
				70		800		
23 April				80	10	800	100	1,000
26 April	50	12	600				150	1,600
29 April				60	10	600	90	1,000

(ii)   *Stores ledger card – LIFO method:*

Date	Receipts Qty	Price £	Value £	Issues Qty	Price £	Value £	Balance Qty	Value £
1 April							40	400
4 April	140	11	1,540				180	1,940
10 April				90	11	990	90	950
12 April	60	12	720				150	1,670

Date	Receipts			Issues			Balance	
	Qty	Price £	Value £	Qty	Price £	Value £	Qty	Value £
13 April				60	12	720		
				40	11	440		
				100		1,160	50	510
16 April	200	10	2,000				250	2,510
21 April				70	10	700	180	1,810
23 April				80	10	800	100	1,010
26 April	50	12	600				150	1,610
				50	12	600		
29 April				10	10	100		
				60		700	90	910

(b) Cost of material used in April: LIFO – £4,260; FIFO – £4,350

(c) See the Appendix to Chapter 3 for a description of the weighted average method. With this method the issue price is determined by dividing the total value by the number of units in stock. This will tend to smooth out price fluctuations and the closing stock valuation will fall between that resulting from the FIFO and LIFO methods. In times of rising prices the cost of sales figure will be higher than FIFO but lower than LIFO.

Answer to question 3.10

(a) (i) *FIFO method:*

		Receipts		Issue		Balance	
		Qty	£	Qty	£	Qty	£
1/6/93	Balance b/f					1,000	4,000
3/6/93	Receipts	2,000	10,000			3,000	14,000
6/6/93	Receipts	1,500	8,250			4,500	22,250
6/6/93	Issues			1,000 at £4 1,500 at £5 = 11,500		2,000	10,750
12/6/93	Receipts	3,000	13,500			5,000	24,250
14/6/93	Issues			500 at £5 1,500 at £5.50 = 17,500 1,500 at £4.50		1,500	6,750

(ii) *LIFO method:*

1/6/93	Balance b/f					1,000	4,000
3/6/93	Receipts	2,000	10,000			3,000	14,000
6/6/93	Receipts	1,500	8,250			4,500	22,250
9/6/93	Issues			1,500 at £5.50 = 13,250 1,000 at £5		2,000	9,000
12/6/93	Receipts	3,000	13,500			5,000	22,500
14/6/93	Issues			3,000 at £4.50 = 16,000 500 at £5		1,500	6,500

(iii) *Weighted average method:*

1/6/93	Balance b/f				1,000 at £4 = £4,000	
3/6/93	Receipts	2,000	10,000		3,000 at £4.667 = £14,000	
6/6/93	Receipts	1,500	8,250		4,500 at £4.944 = £22,250	
9/6/93	Issues			2,500 at £4.944 = £12,361	2,000 at £4.944 = £9,889	
12/6/93	Receipts	3,000	13,500		5,000 at £4.678 = £23,389	
14/6/93	Issues			3,500 at £4.678 = £16,373	1,500 at £4.678 = £7,016	

(b) To answer parts (b) and (c) you should have completed Chapter 16.

(i) $EOQ = \sqrt{2DO/H} = \sqrt{\dfrac{2 \times 80,000 \times 100}{0.25}} = 8,000$ units

(ii) Average stock $= 8,000/2 = 4,000$ units

(iii) Number of orders $= 80,000/8,000 = 10$

(c) 'Buffer stocks' is another term used to refer to safety stocks. See the section on safety stocks in Chapter 16 for an explanation of this term. For an explanation of lead time see the section on determining when to place the order in Chapter 16.

A just-in-time stock policy aims to eliminate buffer (safety) stocks and lead time by making arrangements with suppliers for new stocks to be supplied at frequent intervals at the point where the previous stocks run out.

Answer to question 3.14

Current situation:

Sales		2,500
Wages (£6 per unit)	600	
Materials	500	
Fixed overhead		
£10 per unit)	1,000	2,100
Profit		400

Proposed situation:

Sales		5,000
Wages (£9 per unit)	1,800	
Materials	1,000	
Fixed overhead		
(£5 per unit)	1,000	3,800
Profit		1,200

Incremented approach:

Extra sales		2,500
Extra labour	1,200	
Extra materials	500	1,700
Extra profit		800

The aim of the question is to illustrate that an incentive scheme may increase the wages cost per unit, but this may be offset by a decline in fixed overhead per unit. Also, as long as the increase in wages still provides a contribution to fixed overheads and profit, it may be better to obtain a larger output at a lower unit contribution than a lower output at a larger unit contribution. It is also necessary to consider behavioural factors which cannot be quantified.

For example, an incentive scheme assumes a traditional organizational theory approach and may encourage some of the consequences which behavioural scientists claim are inherent in this theory.

Answer to question 3.16

(i) *Piecework system:*

Output level	80 units	120 units	210 units
Time rate wage	£44	£44	£44
Guaranteed earnings (80%)	£35.20	£35.20	£35.20
Piecework earnings at			
£0.30 per unit	£24	£36	£63
Wage payment	£35.20	£36	£63

(ii) *Bonus system:*

	4 hours	6 hours	10.5 hours
Time allowed	4 hours	6 hours	10.5 hours
Time taken	8 hours	8 hours	8 hours
Time saved	–	–	2.5 hours
Bonus hours (75 %)	_	_	1.875 hours
Bonus payment at £5.50 per hour			£10.31
Time rate wage	£44	£44	£44.00
Total payment	£44	£44	£54.31

Answer to question 3.21

(a) *Calculation of gross wages:*

	Direct		Indirect	
	£		£	
Ordinary hours	15,228	(4230 × £3.60)	1,848	(880 × £2.10)
Overtime premium	756	(630 × $\frac{1}{3}$ × £3.60)	56	(80 × $\frac{1}{3}$ × £2.10)
	15,984		1,904	

Total wages = £17,888 (£15,984 + £1,904)

Allocation of gross wages:

Direct workers' production time: 3,525 hours		£
	(2,400 + 1,125) at £3.60 =	12,690
Direct workers' non-production down time: 705 hours at £3.60	=	2,538
Direct workers' overtime premium	=	756
Indirect workers' gross wages	=	1,904
Wages charged to production overhead	=	5,198

Wages control account:

	£		£
Cash (net wages paid question)	12,864	WIP a/c	12,690
Employees deduction	1,420	Production a/c	5,198
(Balance)	3,604		
	17,888		17,888

(b) (i) The effect of the proposed scheme is examined by comparing the previous week's earnings for the direct workers with the earnings that would have been earned if the proposed scheme had been in operation:

Proposed scheme:

	£
Type 1 receiver (4,800 units at £1.90)	9,120
Type 2 receiver (1,500 units at £2.85)	4,275
Non-productive down time[a]	1,410
	14,805

Present scheme:
    Direct wages paid per part (a)   £15,984

Note:
[a]Calculation of allowed hours for the previous weeks' production:

Type 1	4,800 units $\times$ 24 minutes	1,920 hours	
Type 2	1,500 units $\times$ 36 minutes	900 hours	
		2,820 hours	

Non-productive down time = 20% $\times$ 2,820 hours $\times$£2.5 = £1,410.

Conclusion:

It appears that the proposed incentive scheme will reduce the wages cost, but the factors outlined in (ii) must be examined before a final decision is made. The above analysis assumes that the company will pay only for the hours worked by the direct operatives. If hours which are surplus to requirements are paid then the results of the proposed scheme should be adjusted as follows:

	Hours
Total productive hours per note *a* above	2,820
Allowance for non-productive time (20%)	564
	3,384
Ordinary time for direct operatives	3,600
Shortfall	216

Assuming that the 216 hours are paid at £2.50 or £3.60, the cost of the incentive scheme will be increased by the appropriate amount. However, the proposed scheme is still cheaper than the present scheme.

(ii)   Additional factors to be examined are:

    (a)   How will any surplus plus labour capacity (as in (i)) be dealt with?

    (b)   Will the opportunity for the direct workers to earn a higher wage be a source of grievance with the indirect workers and workers in other departments?

    (c)   Will product quality be affected?

    (d)   Will less supervision be required?

    (e)   Will the scheme result in increased administration costs?

    (f)   Will future output be significantly increased, and can it be sold? An estimate of future output with the incentive scheme and output without the incentive scheme is required. Cost and revenue comparison should then be made for the different output levels.

    (g)   Will variable overheads be affected? Do they vary with direct labour hours of input?

Accounting for overhead expenditure

Answers to Chapter 4

Question summary

4.1 to 4.4
Multiple choice questions.

4.5 to 4.7
Discussion questions relating to Chapter 4.

4.8 to 4.13
Questions which require the apportionment of overheads, the preparation of overhead analysis statements and the calculation of departmental overhead rates. Questions 4.8, 4.10, 4.11 and 4.13 also require the calculation of product costs. Part (d) of Question 4.13 requires the preparation of an overhead control account. This topic is dealt with in Chapter 5.

4.14
Job cost calculation.

4.15 to 4.22
Calculation and discussion of different overhead absorption rates. Questions 4.16 to 4.19 also require the calculation of under-/over-recovery of overheads. In addition, Question 4.18 requires an analysis of the under-/over-recovery of overheads and a discussion of predetermined versus actual overhead rates. Question 4.20 involves the reallocation of service department overheads and 4.21 requires the separation of fixed and variable overheads using the high-low method.

4.23
Calculation of overhead absorption rates and product costs and a make-or-buy decision.

4.24 to 4.27
Reapportionment of service department costs. Question 4.25 also requires a product cost calculation and the selection of the most suitable overhead recovery method.

4.28

Requires the calculation of overhead absorption rates and extraction of variable costs for a make-or-buy decision. This question is useful for emphasizing the decision-making aspects at this stage. Alternatively you may prefer to defer this problem until make-or-buy decisions have been studied in Chapter 10.

Answer to question 4.5

(a) For the answer to this question see the section on predetermined overhead rates in Chapter 4.

(b) A lower production overhead rate does not necessarily indicate that factory X is more efficient than factory Y. The reasons for this are:
  (i) Factory Y's operations might be highly mechanized, resulting in large depreciation costs, whereas factory X's operations might be labour-intensive. Consequently products produced in factory Y will incur higher overhead and lower labour costs, whereas products produced in factory X will incur lower overhead and higher labour costs.
  (ii) Factory Y may have invested in plant with a larger operating capacity in order to meet future output. This will result in larger fixed costs and a higher overhead rate.
  (iii) Both factories may use different denominators in calculating the overhead rates. For example, if factory Y uses normal capacity and factory X uses maximum practical capacity then factory Y will have a higher overhead rate.
  (iv) Current budgeted activity might be used by both firms to calculate the overhead rate. The level of budgeted sales will determine budgeted activity. The lower overhead rate of factory X might be due to a higher sales volume rather than efficient factory operations.
  (v) Different cost classification might result in different overhead rates. Factory X might treat all expenditure as a direct cost wherever possible. For example, employers' costs might be charged out by means of an inflated hourly wage rate. Factory Y may treat such items as overhead costs.

Answer to question 4.6

(a) For the answer to this question see the section on blanket overhead rates in Chapter 4.

(b) For the answer to this question see Appendix 4.2 to Chapter 4.

Answer to question 4.7

See Chapter 4 (sections on overheads for decision-making and control) and Question 4.28 for the answer to this question.

Answer to question 4.8

(a)

	Production department			Service department	Total
	A £	B £	C £	£	£
Direct	261,745	226,120	93,890	53,305	635,060
Indirect	135,400 (40%)	118,475 (35%)	67,700 (20%)	16,925 (5%)	338,500
Service dept apportionment	23,410 ($\frac{1}{3}$)	23,410 ($\frac{1}{3}$)	23,410 ($\frac{1}{3}$)	(70,230)	
	420,555	368,005	185,000	—	973,560
Allocation base (1)	17,760 = £23.68 per direct labour hour	5,760 = £63.89 per m/c hour	148,000 = £1.25 per hour		

Note:

1. Dept. A direct labour hours
   $= 10 \times 37 \times 48$
   $= 17,760$
   Dept. B machine hours
   $= 5 \times 24 \times 48$
   $= 5,760$
   Dept. C units
   $= 148,000$

(b)

	£
Dept A	
9 direct labour hours at £23.68	213.12
Dept B	
3 m/c hours at £63.89	191.67
Dept C	
100 units at £1.25	125.00
	529.79

Cost per unit = £5.30 (£529.79/100)

Answer to question 4.9

(a) *Overhead analysis sheet:*

Expense	Apportionment basis	Machining £	Assembly £	Finishing £	Total £
Indirect wages/salaries	Allocated	120,354	238,970	89,700	449,024
Rent	Area	5,708,475	4,439,925	2,537,100	12,685,500
Business rates	Area	1,552,905	1,207,815	690,180	3,450,900
Heat/light	Area	443,408	344,872	197,070	985,350
Machine power	Horsepower	1,878,890	72,265	939,445	2,890,600
Plant ~~department~~	Value of plant	375,000	45,000	180,000	600,000
Canteen subsidy	No. of employees	100,000	120,000	36,000	256,000
Total		10,179,032	6,468,847	4,669,495	21,317,374

Dep oV

(b) Most of the overheads in the machine department are likely to be machine related and therefore it is appropriate to use a machine hour rate. The machine hour cost rate is also used for the finishing department, because machine hours are the predominant activity. Similar arguments can be used to justify the use of a direct labour hour overhead rate in the assembly department. The overhead rates are as follows:

Machining $\dfrac{£10,179,032}{200,000} = £50.90$ per machine hour

Assembly $\dfrac{£6,468,847}{140,000} = £46.21$ per direct labour hour

Finishing $\dfrac{£4,669,847}{90\,000} = £51.88$ per machine hour

Answer to question 4.12

(a) *Overhead analysis sheet:*

| | Total £ | Production | | | Service | | |
		Cutting £	Tents £	Bags £	Stores £	Canteen £	Maintenance £
Indirect wages	147,200	6,400	19,500	20,100	41,200	15,000	45,000
Consumable materials	54,600	5,300	4,100	2,300	–	18,700	24,200
Plant depreciation	84,200	31,200	17,500	24,600	2,500	3,400	5,000
Power[a]	31,700	5,389	12,046	10,144	951	2,536	634
Heat and light[b]	13,800						
Rent and rates[b]	14,400	11,120	13,900	9,730	2,085	3,475	1,390
Building insurance[b]	13,500						
	359,400	59,409	67,046	66,874	46,736	43,111	76,224
Reapportionment:							
Stores[c]	–	29,210	5,842	5,842	(46,736)	–	5,842
Canteen[d]	–	2,694	18,476	21,941		(43,111)	–
Maintenance[e]	–	1,887	37,731	42,448			(82,066)
	359,400	93,200	129,095	137,105			
Machine hours	87,000	2,000	40,000	45,000			
Labour hours	112,000	7,000	48,000	57,000			
Machine hour rate		£46.60	£3.23	£3.05			
Overheads per labour hour		£13.31	£2.69	£2.41			

Notes:

Bases of apportionment: ^{a} estimated power usage; ^{b} area; ^{c} value of issues; ^{d} direct labour hours; ^{e} machine hours. Actual basis for other costs.

(b) See the section on predetermined overhead rates in Chapter 4 for the answer to this question. In addition the following points should be made:

    (i) It draws attention to the under-/over-recovery of overheads arising from changes in production levels.

    (ii) There is difficulty in determining estimated overheads and an appropriate level of activity when calculating predetermined overhead rates.

Answer to question 4.15

(a) Percentage of direct labour cost method = (£600,000/£200,000) × 100

                             = 300% of direct labour cost

    Direct labour hour method = (£600,000/40,000 direct labour hours)

                             = £15 per direct labour hour

    Machine hour method   = (£600,000/50,000 machine hour)

                             = £12 per machine hour

(b) See the section on predetermined overhead rates in Chapter 4 for the answer to this question.

(c) The question states that the company has become machine-intensive and implies that in the long term there is a closer association between overhead expenditure and machine hours than the other two methods. Therefore the best measure of overhead resources consumed by jobs or products is machine hours.

(d) *Job Ax:*

	£
Direct material	3,788
Direct labour	1,100
Direct expenses	422
Prime cost	5,310
Production overhead (120 machine hours × £12)	1,440
Factory cost	6,750
Administrative overheads (20% × £6,750)	1,350
Total cost	8,100
Profit (£8,100/0.90 − £8,100)	900
Selling price	9,000

Workings:

Administration overhead absorption rate = Total admin. overheads/total factory cost

                                        = £328,000/£1,640,000

                                        = 20% of factory cost

(e) The general characteristics of incentive schemes should ensure that:

    (i) the scheme is simple to understand and administer;

    (ii) payment should be made as quickly as possible after production;

    (iii) there should be no limit on earnings and employees must be safeguarded from earning lower wages than time rate wages arising from problems which are outside their control.

The advantages of incentive schemes are:

    (i) increased production and lower average unit costs;

    (ii) increased morale of the workforce;

    (iii) attraction of more efficient workers to the company.

Answer to question 4.17

(a) Predetermined machine hour rate = $\dfrac{\text{machine department overheads (£1,080,000)}}{\text{machine hours (80,000)}}$

Machining department = £13.50 per machine hour
Hand finishing department = £760,000/120,000 labour hours
= £6.33 per labour hour

(b) (i)

	Machine department £	Hand finishing department £
Overhead incurred	84,500	67,100
Overhead absorbed	81,000 (6,000 × £13.50)	60,800 (9,600 × £6.33)
Under recovery of overheads	3,500	6,300

(ii) Overheads that are apportioned to cost centres tend to be on an arbitrary basis and are unlikely to be controllable by the cost centre manager. Managers should be held accountable for only those overheads that they can control. See the section on responsibility accounting and guidelines for reporting in Chapter 14 for a more detailed discussion of controllable and non-controllable costs.

(c) Absorption costing is used by companies to ensure that all products/services bear an equitable share of company overheads. The Statement of Standard Accounting Practice (SSAP 9) requires that stocks should be valued at full production cost. Therefore absorption costing is required to allocate overheads to products in order to meet financial accounting requirements.

Answer to question 4.19

(a) (i) Percentage of direct materials = $\dfrac{\text{production overhead}}{\text{direct materials}} \times 100$

$= \dfrac{£300,000}{£100,000} \times 100 = 300\%$

(ii) Percentage of direct wages $= \dfrac{\text{production overhead}}{\text{direct wages}} \times 100$

$= \dfrac{£300,000}{£50,000} \times 100 = 600\%$

(iii) Percentage of prime cost $= \dfrac{\text{production overhead}}{\text{prime cost}} \times 100$

$= \dfrac{£300,000}{£150,000} \times 100 = 200\%$

(iv) Units of output $= \dfrac{\text{production overhead}}{\text{units}}$

$= \dfrac{£300,000}{300} = £1,000 \text{ per unit}$

$$\text{(v)} \quad \text{Labour hour rate} = \frac{\text{production overhead}}{\text{labour hours}}$$

$$= \frac{£300,000}{25,000} = £12 \text{ per hour}$$

$$\text{(vi)} \quad \text{Machine hour rate} = \frac{\text{production overhead}}{\text{machine hours}}$$

$$= \frac{£300,000}{15,000} = £20 \text{ per hour}$$

(b) The answer to this question is explained in Appendix 4.2 to Chapter 4.

(c)

	(i) Percentage of direct materials £	(ii) Percentage of direct wages £	(iii) Percentage of prime cost £	(iv) Units of output £	(v) Labour hour rate £	(vi) Machine hour rate £
Direct materials	250	250	250	250	250	250
Direct wages	200	200	200	200	200	200
Prime cost	450	450	450	450	450	450
Production overhead	750^a	1,200^b	900^c	1,000^d	960^e	1,000^f
Total cost	1,200	1,650	1,350	1,450	1,410	1,450

Notes:
^{a} £250 × 300%
^{b} £200 × 600%
^{c} £450 × 200%
^{d} 1 unit of output at £1,000
^{e} 80 direct labour hours at £12 per hour
^{f} 50 machine hours at £20 per hour

Answer to question 4.20

(a) In order to ascertain the actual overhead traced to the production departments, it is necessary to allocate the service department overheads to the filling and sealing departments:

	Filling £	Sealing £	Maintenance £	Canteen £
Allocated	74,260	38,115	25,050	24,375
Reallocation of:				
Canteen	14,625 (60%)	7,800 (32%)	1,950 (8%)	(24,375)
Maintenance	18,900 (70%)	7,290 (27%)	(27,000)	810 (3%)
Canteen	486 (60%)	259 (32%)	65 (8%)	(810)
Maintenance	47 (70/97)	18 (27/97)	–	–
	108,318	53,482		

Predetermined overhead rates:

	Filling £	Sealing £
Budgeted overheads	110,040	53,300
Budgeted direct labour hours	13,100	10,250
Direct labour hour overhead rate	8.40	5.20
Overhead incurred	108,318	53,482
Overhead allocated	107,688 (12,820 × £8.40)	52,390 (10,075 × £5.20)
(Under-)/over-recovery	(630)	(1,092)

The objectives of overhead apportionment and absorption are:

(i) To meet the stock valuation and profit measurement requirements for financial accounting purposes. The statement of standard accounting practice (SSAP 9) requires that all manufacturing overheads be traced to products for stock valuation purposes.

(ii) For various decisions, such as pricing decisions, management require estimates of the total product costs.

(iii) Overhead costs may be traced to different segments of the business, such as product groups or geographical regions, in order to assess the performance of each segment.

Overhead apportionment and absorption can be criticized on the following grounds:

(i) The process includes many arbitrary apportionments and does not provide an accurate indication of the resources consumed by each product. In tracing overheads to products, the allocation procedure assumes that all overheads are related to volume. This is inappropriate for many fixed overheads, since they are fixed in the short term, and tend to be caused by factors other than volume, such as the diversity of the product range, number of set-ups and range of component parts which the firm stocks.

(ii) Fixed overheads are sunk costs, and will tend not to change in the short term. Hence they are unaffected in the short term, irrespective of which decisions are taken. Arbitrary overhead allocations should not be used for decision-making purposes.

(iii) Overhead allocations are normally undertaken for stock valuation purposes. The procedures are not intended to meet other requirements, such as decision-making and performance evaluation.

(iv) Individuals should not be held accountable for costs which they cannot control. Arbitrary apportionment of overheads is therefore inappropriate for cost control and performance measurement purposes.

Answer to question 4.22

(a) (i) An over-absorption of overheads occurs because the actual overheads charged to products (or cleints) exceeds the overheads incurred. Therefore £747,360 (£742,600 actual overheads + £4,760 over-absorption) were charged to clients during the period. Because overheads are charged on the basis of actual direct hours worked, the actual professional staff hours worked during the period were 99,648 (£747,360/£7.50 hourly overhead rate). Therefore budgeted professional staff hours = 98,288 (99,648 − 1,360).

(ii) Budgeted overhead expenditure
$$= \text{Budgeted hours } (98,288) \times \text{Overhead rate } (£7.50)$$
$$= £737,160$$

(b) To determine the overhead rate the senior staff hours should be weighted by a factor of 1.4 and the junior staff hours by a factor of 1.0:

Senior staff $= 21,600 \times 1.4 = 30,240$
Junior staff $= 79,300 \times 1.0 = \underline{79,300}$
$\underline{109,540}$

Allocation of overheads:

Senior staff $= 30,240/109,540 \times £784,000 = £216,434$
Junior staff $= 79,300/109,540 \times £784,000 = \underline{£567,566}$
$\underline{£784,000}$

Senior staff overhead allocation rate $= £216,434/21,600$ hours
$= £10.020$ per hour
Junior staff overhead allocation rate $= £567,566/79,300$ hours
$= £7.157$ per hour

(c) Presumably the senior staff consume a greater proportion of the overhead costs than the junior staff and the revised method is an attempt to reflect this difference in resource consumption. For example, senior staff are likely to require more office space and make greater demands on secretarial time, telephones etc. The revised method creates two separate cost centres and overhead rates whereas the previous method used a single blanket rate for the whole organization.

(d) See the section on under- and over-recovery of overheads in Chapter 4 for the answer to this question. Differences between overhead incurred and overhead absorbed may be due to:

(1) Differences between actual and budgeted expenditure
(2) Differences between actual and budgeted activity level

Answer to question 4.26

(a) (i)

	Machining £		Finishing £		Assembly £		Materials handling £		Inspection £	
Initial cost	400,000		200,000		100,000		100,000		50,000	
Reapportion:										
Materials handling	30,000		25,000		35,000		(100,000)		10,000	
	430,000		225,000		135,000		–		60,000	
Inspection	12,000	(20%)	18,000	(30%)	27,000	(45%)	3,000	(5%)	(60,000)	
	442,000		243,000		162,000		3,000		–	
Materials handling	900	(30%)	750	(25%)	1,050	(45%)	(3,000)		300	(10%)
	442,900		243,750		163,050		–		300	
Inspection	60	(20%)	90	(30%)	135	(45%)	15	(5%)	(300)	
	442,960		243,840		163,185		(15)		–	
	5		4		6					
	442,965		243,844		163,191					

(ii) Let
$x = $ material handling
$y = $ inspection
$x = 100,000 + 0.05y$
$y = 50,000 + 0.1x$

Rearranging the above equations:

$$x - 0.05y = 100,000 \tag{1}$$

$$-0.1x + y = 50,000 \tag{2}$$

Multiply equation (1) by 1 and equation (2) by 10:

$$x - 0.05y = 100,000$$
$$-x + 10y = 500,000$$

Adding the above equations:

$$9.95y = 600,000$$
$$y = 60,301$$

Substituting for y in equation (1):

$$x - 0.05 \times 60,301 = 100,000$$
$$x = 103,015$$

x

Apportioning the values of x and y to the production departments in the agreed percentages:

		Machining (£)		Finishing (£)		Assembly (£)
Initial cost		400,000		200,000		100,000
(x) Materials handling	(0.3)	30,905	(0.25)	25,754	(0.35)	36,055
(y) Inspection	(0.2)	12,060	(0.3)	18,090	(0.45)	27,136
		442,965		243,844		163,191

(b) Reapportioning production service department costs is necessary to compute product costs for stock valuation purposes in order to meet the requirements of SSAP 9. However, it is questionable whether arbitrary apportionments of fixed overhead costs provides useful information for decision-making. Such apportionments are made to meet stock valuation requirements, and they are inappropriate for decision-making, cost control and performance reporting.

An alternative treatment would be to adopt a variable costing system and treat fixed overheads as period costs. This would eliminate the need to reapportion service department fixed costs. A more recent suggestion is to trace support/service department costs to products using an activity-based costing system (ABCS). For a description of ABCS you should refer to Chapter 11.

(c) For the answer to this question see the section on under- and over-recovery of overheads in Chapter 4.

Answer to question 4.27

(i) With the step-wise method the costs of the first service department (Department G specified in the question) are reapportioned to the second department but return allocations are not made from the second department back to the first department.

	Production depts			Internal services	
	1	2		G	H
	£000	£000		£000	£000
Overheads	870	690	Costs	160	82
G apportioned	96 (60%)	48 (30%)		−160	16 (10%)
					98
H apportioned	61 ($^{50}/_{80}$)	37 ($^{30}/_{80}$)			−98
	1,027	775			

(ii) Let G = Service Department G overheads
Let H = Service Department H overheads

$$G = 160 + 0.2H$$
$$H = 82 + 0.1G$$

Rearranging the above equations

$$-0.2H + G = 160 \qquad (1)$$
$$1H - 0.1G = 82 \qquad (2)$$

Multiply equation (1) by 1 and equation (2) by 10

$$-0.2H + G = 160$$
$$10H - G = 820$$

Add the above equations together:

$$9.8H = 980$$
$$H = 100$$

Substituting for the value of H in equation (1)

$$-0.2(100) + G = 160$$
$$G = 180$$

Internal	Total		Production depts 1		2
	£000		£000		£000
G (180 × 90%)	162	($\frac{6}{9}$)	108	($\frac{3}{9}$)	54
H (100 × 80%)	80	($\frac{5}{8}$)	50	($\frac{3}{8}$)	30
	242				
Overheads (given)			158		84
			870		690
			1,028		774

(iii) The simultaneous equation method will yield more accurate allocations because it takes into account the fact that service departments serve each other whereas the step-wise method ignores such reciprocal usage. The step-wise method involves simpler computations and, in this question, does not give a significantly different answer. However, the step-wise method may yield inaccurate results where service costs are high and there are more than two service departments with significantly different usage ratios between the departments.

(a) The calculations of the overhead absorption rates are:

Forming department machine hour rate = £6.15 per machine hour
(£602,700 ÷ 98,000 hours)
Finishing department labour hour rate = £2.25 per labour hour
(£346,500 ÷ 154,000 hours)

The forming department is mechanized and it is likely that a significant proportion of overheads will be incurred as a consequence of employing and running the machines. Therefore a machine hour rate has been used. In the finishing department several grades of labour are used. Consequently, the direct wages percentage method is inappropriate and the direct labour hour method should be used.

(b) The decision should be based on a comparison of the incremental cost with the purchase price of an outside supplier if spare capacity exists. If no spare capacity exists then the lost contribution on displaced work must be considered. The calculation of incremental costs requires that the variable element of the total overhead absorption rate must be calculated. The calculation is:

Forming department variable machine hour rate
= £2.05 per hour (£200,900 ÷ 98,000 hours)
Finishing department variable direct labour hour rate
= £0.75 per hour (£115,500 ÷ 154,000 hours)

The calculation of the variable costs per unit of each component is:

	A	B	C
	£	£	£
Prime cost	24.00	31.00	29.00
Variable overheads: Forming	8.20	6.15	4.10
Finishing	2.25	7.50	1.50
Variable unit manufacturing cost	34.45	44.65	34.60
Purchase price	30	65	60

On the basis of the above information component A should be purchased and components B and C manufactured. This decision is based on the assumption that:
  (i) variable overheads vary in proportion to machine hours (forming department) and direct labour hours (finishing department);
  (ii) fixed overheads remain unaffected by any changes in activity;
  (iii) space capacity exists.
For a discussion of make-or-buy decisions see Chapter 10.

(c) Production overhead absorption rates are calculated in order to ascertain costs per unit of output for stock valuation and profit measurement purposes. Such costs are inappropriate for decision-making and cost control. For an explanation of this see the sections on overheads for decision-making and overheads for control in Chapter 4.

Accounting entries for a job costing system

Answers to Chapter 5

Question summary

5.1 and 5.2
Multiple choice questions.

5.3 to 5.5
Preparation of ledger accounts for an integrated accounting system.

5.6 to 5.8
Preparation of ledger accounts for an interlocking accounting system. Question 5.7 also includes a reconciliation of the cost accounts with the financial accounts and 5.8 requires the preparation of accounts from incomplete information.

5.9 and 5.10
Reconciliation of the cost and financial accounts.

5.11
Preparation of cost ledger accounts where extracts from the financial accounts and the reconciliation of the costing and financial accounting profit are given in the question.

5.12
Stores pricing on a weighted average basis and the preparation of the raw materials and finished goods accounts.

5.13 and 5.14
Preparation of journal entries for payroll and labour cost accounting.

5.15 and 5.16
Preparation of the wages control accounts. Question 5.15 also requires the analysis of gross wages and the preparation of the Overhead Control Account.

5.17 to 5.20
Preparation of contract accounts.

Answer to question 5.4

(a) and (b)

Fixed assets

	(£000)		
Balance b/f	275		

Share capital

			(£000)
		Balance b/f	500

Creditors control

Bank	150	Stores control	525
Balance c/f	487.5	Production overhead control	47.5
		Production overhead control	26
		Production overhead control	39
	637.5		637.5
		Balance b/f	487.5

Provision for depreciation

			(£000)
		Production overhead control	15

Bank

	(£000)		(£000)
Balance b/f	225	Wages control	500
Debtors	520	Production overhead control	20
		Sales overhead control	40
		Administration overhead control	25
		Creditors control	150
		Balance c/f	10
	745		745
Balance b/f	10		

Wages control

	(£000)		(£000)
Bank	500	WIP: Department A	300
Wage deductions	175	WIP: Department B	260
		Production overhead control	42.5
		Sales overhead control	47.5
		Administration overhead control	25
	675		675

Wage deductions

			(£000)
		Wages control	175

Stores control

	(£000)		
Creditors control	525	WIP: Department A	180
		WIP: Department B	192.5
		Production overhead control	65
		Balance c/f	87.5
	525		525
Balance b/f	87.5		

ACCOUNTING ENTRIES FOR A JOB COSTING SYSTEM

Production overhead control

	(£000)		(£000)
Creditors control	47.5	WIP control: Department A	110
Bank	20	WIP control: Department B	120
Stores control	65	Profit and loss	25
Wages control	42.5		
Creditors control	26		
Creditors control	39		
Provision for depreciation	15		
	255		255

WIP control: Department A

	(£000)		(£000)
Stores control	180	Finished goods control	570
Wages control	300	Balance c/f	20
Production overhead control	110		
	590		590
Balance b/f	20		

WIP control: Department B

	(£000)		(£000)
Stores control	192.5	Finished goods control	555
Wages control	260	Balance c/f	17.5
Production overhead control	120		
	572.5		572.5
Balance b/f	17.5		

Selling overhead control

	(£000)		(£000)
Bank	40	Profit and loss	87.5
Wages control	47.5		
	87.5		87.5

Admininistration overhead control

	(£000)		(£000)
Bank	25	Profit and loss	50
Wages control	25		
	50		50

Debtors control

	(£000)		(£000)
Sales	870	Bank	520
		Balance c/f	350
	870		870
Balance b/f	350		

Finished goods control

	(£000)		(£000)
WIP Control:		Cost sales	700
Department A	570	Balance c/f	425
WIP Control:			
Department B	555		
	1125		1125
Balance b/f	425		

Cost of sales

	(£000)		(£000)
Finished goods control	700	Profit and loss	700
	700		700

Sales

	(£000)		(£000)
Profit and loss	870	Debtors	870

(c) (i)   *Profit statement for the period 1 February to 30 April:*

	(£000)	(£000)
Sales		870
Cost of sales		700
Gross profit		170
Under-absorption of production overheads	25	
Selling overheads	87.5	
Admininistration overheads	50	162.5
Net profit		7.5

(ii)   *Balance sheet as at 30 April:*

	(£000)	(£000)	(£000)
Fixed assets at cost			275
Provision for depreciation			15
Written down value			260
Current assets			
Stock: Finished goods		425	
WIP: Department A	20		
WIP: Department B	17.5	37.5	
Raw materials		87.5	
		550	
Debtors		350	
Bank		10	
		910	
Current liabilities			
Creditors	487.5		
Wage deductions	175	662.5	247.5
			507.5
Financed:			
Capital			500
Profit			7.5
			507.5

Answer to question 5.6

(a)

Stores control

	£		£
Balance b/d	54,250		
Direct material purchases			
(Cost Control a/c)	216,590	Work-in-progress	197,750
		Balance c/d	73,090
	270,840		270,840
Balance b/d	73,090		

Work-in-progress control

	£		£
Balance b/d	89,100		
Stores control	197,750	Finished goods control	512,050
Direct wages	85,480		
Production overhead			
control	213,700		
		Balance c/d	73,980
	586,030		586,030
Balance b/d	73,980		

Finished goods control

	£		£
Balance b/d	42,075		
Work-in-progress	512,050	Cost of sales	493,460
		Balance c/d	60,665
	554,125		554,125
Balance b/d	60,665		

Production overhead control

	£		£
Cost Control a/c	208,220	Work-in-progress	213,700
Additional depreciation	12,500	(250% × £85,480)	
		Balance to Profit and Loss a/c	7,020
		(Under-absorbed overhead)	
	220,720		220,720

(b) The balance on the production overhead control account represents the under-absorption of production overheads. The balance is transferred to the profit and loss account.

(c) Stocks may be valued on a variable costing basis for internal profit measurement whereas for external financial accounting stocks must be valued on an absorption costing basis. Because stocks are part of the cost of goods sold calculation, the profits will differ in the financial and cost accounts. Sometimes for decision-making it is appropriate to include imputed costs that do not involve cash outlays. Examples of imputed costs include notional costs such as the notional rent for the use of a building that is owned. The notional

ANSWER TO QUESTION 5.6

rent represents an opportunity cost of the rent from the alternative use of the buildings that ought to be taken into account for decision-making. Incorporating notional expenses in the cost accounts will result in the cost accounts reporting a smaller profit than the financial accounts. Items such as profit and losses on the sale of assets and debenture interest paid are not recorded in the cost accounts whereas these items are recorded in the financial accounts. Therefore the inclusion of these items in the financial accounts will result in a difference in profits between the financial and cost accounts.

Answer to question 5.8

(a) See the comparison between management accounting and financial accounting in Chapter 1 for the answer to this question.

(b) Note that the job ledger control account shown in the question is equivalent to the work in progress control account described in Chapter 5.

Stores ledger control account

	(£000)		(£000)
Opening balance	176.0	Job ledger control A/c	
Financial ledger		(64,500 kg × £3.20)	206.4
control A/c	224.2	Production o'head control	
		A/c (Balancing figure)	24.3
		Closing balance	169.5
	400.2		400.2

Production wages control account

	(£000)		(£000)
Financial ledger		Job ledger control A/c (75%)	147.0
control A/c	196.0	Production o'head control	
		A/c (25%)	49.0
	196.0		196.0

Production overhead control account

	(£000)		(£000)
Financial ledger		Job ledger control A/c (1)	191.1
control A/c	119.3	Under-absorbed overhead	
Stores ledger control A/c	24.3	(Balance to profit and loss	
Production wages control		A/c)	1.5
A/c	49.0		
	192.6		192.6

Job ledger control account

	(£000)		(£000)
Opening balance	114.9	Cost of sales A/c (balancing	
Stores ledger control A/c	206.4	figure)	506.4
Production wages control		Closing balance	153.0
A/c	147.0		
Production o'head			
control A/c	191.1		
	659.4		659.4

Note:

(1)   Direct labour hours $= \dfrac{\text{Direct labour wages (£147,000)}}{\text{Direct labour wage rate (£5)}} = 29,400$ hours

     Overhead charged to production = 29,400 direct labour hours $\times$ direct labour hour rate (£6.50) = £191,100.

Answer to question 5.10

	£	£
Profit as per financial accounts:		80,000
Add: Debenture interest (1)	30,000	
Discount allowed (1)	35,000	
Loss on machine (1)	20,000	
Overheads	30,000	115,000
Less: Notional rent (2)	12,000	
Dividends received (1)	20,000	(32,000)
Stock differences:		
Raw materials opening stock	(2,000)	
Finished goods opening stock	2,000	
Raw materials closing stock	5,000	
Finished goods closing stock	4,000	9,000
Profit as per cost accounts		172,000

Notes:

(1)   Financial expenses which are recorded in the financial accounts but not the cost accounts.

(2)   Notional rent charge which is recorded in the cost accounts but not the financial accounts.

Answer to question 5.14

(a)   The costs of labour turnover include:

    (i)   leaving costs associated with completing the appropriate documentation and lost production if the employees cannot be immediately replaced;

    (ii)   recruitment costs resulting from the advertising, selection and engagement of new staff;

    (iii)   learning costs including training costs, the cost arising from lower productivity and defective work during the learning period.

(b)   *Workings:*

    Basic time = 40 workers $\times$ 38 hours per week for 4 weeks = 6,080 hours

    Overtime = Total hours (6,528) $-$ Basic time (6,080) = 448 hours

	£
Total wages = Basic pay (6,528 hours $\times$ £4)	= 26,112
Overtime premium (448 hours $\times$ £1.40)	627.20
	26,739.20
Less deductions (30% $\times$ £26,739.20)	8,021.76
Net amount paid	18,717.44

Cost of productive time
$$(6{,}528 \text{ hours} - 188 \text{ hours idle time}) \times £4 \qquad 25{,}360$$
$$\text{Cost of idle time } (188 \text{ hours} \times £4) \qquad 752$$

Journal entries:

	Dr.	Cr.
Wages control	£26,739.20	
Bank		£18,717.44
Employee deductions		8,021.76
Being analysis of gross wages for direct workers		
Work in progress	£25,360.00	
Production overhead (1)	£1,379.20	
Wages control		£26,739.20
Being the allocation of gross wages for the period		

Note:

(1) Production overhead = Idle time (£752) + Overtime premium (£627.20)

Answer to question 5.16

(a) *Workings:*

Gross wages paid:		£
Direct (25,520 hours × £4.80)		122,496.00
(2,120 overtime hours × £1.44)		3,052.80
		125,548.80
Indirect (4,430 hours × £3.90)		17,277.00
(380 hours × £1.17)		444.60
		17,721.60

Tax and employees' national insurance:		
Direct (£125,548.80 − £97,955)		27,593.80
Indirect (£17,721.60 − £13,859)		3,862.60
		31,456.40

Productive hours (7,200 + 11,600 + 4,400)		23,200 hours
Direct labour unproductive labour hours (25,520 − 23,200)		2,320 hours
Productive hours charged to WIP (23,200 × £4.80)		£111,360.00

Charge to production overhead:

	£	£
Gross wages of indirect workers	17,721.60	
Overtime premium (direct workers)	3,052.80	
Unproductive time of direct workers		
(2,320 × £4.80)	11,136.00	31,910.40

Wages control account

	£		£
Cash/bank (net wages):		WIP	111,360.00
Direct	97,955.00	Production overhead	31,910.40
Indirect	13,859.00		
Tax and national insurance	31,456.40		
	143,270.40		143,270.40

(b) The cost of the proposed piecework scheme based on the production for the current period is as follows:

	£
Product 1 (36,000 units × £1)	36,000.00
2 (116,000 units × £0.50)	58,000.00
3 (52,800 units × £0.40)	21,120.00
	115,120.00
Unproductive time (see note*)	6,766.67
	121,886.67

Calculation of wages paid for unproductive time:
Productive time is:

Product 1 (36,000 units/6 units per hour)	6,000.00 hours
2 (116,000 units/12 units per hour)	9,666.67 hours
3 (52,800 units/14.4 units per hour)	3,666.67 hours
	19,333.34 hours

Wages paid for unproductive time	
(10% × 19,333.34 hours × £3.50)	£6,766.67

The direct labour cost per unit for the current scheme is:
Product 1 (7,200 hours × £4.80)/36,000 units = £0.96
2 (11,600 hours × £4.80)/116,000 units = £0.48
3 (4,400 hours × £4.80)/52,800 units = £0.40

The current piecework rates exceed the above unit costs but the overall costs are lower with the piecework scheme because of less unproductive time and a saving in overtime. It is also likely that overhead costs will be reduced because of a reduction in overtime in respect of indirect labour.

Answer to question 5.19

(a)   *Contract accounts*

	1 £	2 £	3 £		1 £	2 £	3 £
Plant on site	16,000	12,000	8,000	Materials stock c/f	3,000	3,000	1,500
Materials	44,000	41,000	15,000	Cost of work not			
Wages	80,000	74,500	12,000	certified c/f	4,000	6,000	9,000
General expenses	3,000	1,800	700	Plant on site c/f	12,000	10,000	7,500
Central overheads	1,600	1,490	240	Cost of work certified			
Accrued expenses c/f	700	600	600	(balance)	136,300	112,390	18,540
Provision for							
faulty work c/f	10,000						
	155,300	131,390	36,540		155,300	131,390	36,540
Cost of work				Attributable			
certified b/f	136,300	112,390	18,540	sales revenue	145,433	110,000	18,540
Profit taken				Loss taken		2,390	
this period	9,133						
	145,433	112,390	18,540		145,433	112,390	18,540
Cost of work not				Accrued			
certified b/f	4,000	6,000	9,000	expenses b/f	700	600	600
Material stock b/f	3,000	3,000	1,500	Provision for			
Plant on site b/f	12,000	10,000	7,500	faulty work b/f	10,000		

Profit calculations:
Contract 1: ⅔ × £13,700 profit.
Contract 2: The loss to date (£112,390 − £110,000) is written off.

Contract 3: The contract is less than one-third complete. Therefore no profit is taken for the period.

(b) *Balance sheet (extracts):*

	(£)	(£)
Plant on site*ᵃ* (£12,000 + £10,000 + £7,500)		29,500
Raw material stock (£3,000 + £3,000 + £1,500)		7,500
Cost of work completed to date*ᵇ*		
(£140,300 + £118,390 + £27,540)	286,230	
Add profit taken (£9,133 − £2,390)	6,743	
	292,973	
Less progress payments received*ᶜ*		
(£120,000 + £88,000 + £16,000)	224,000	68,973
Accrued expenses (£10,000 + £1,900)		11,900

Notes:
*ᵃ*Closing value of plant on site is calculated as follows:
  Contract 1 = £16,000 − (£16,000/4)
  Contract 2 = £12,000 − (£4,000 annual depreciation for 6 months)
  Contract 3 = £8,000 − (£2,000 annual depreciation for 3 months)
*ᵇ*Note that completed work to date consists of the cost of uncertified work plus the cost of the certified work.
*ᶜ*It is assumed that cash has been received in respect of the invoiced value of work certified.

Answer to question 5.20

(a) (i) *Orders 488 and 517:*
Both orders span two accounting years and are of significant value. They should therefore be treated as long-term contracts.

Orders 518 and 519:
Both orders are of small value and short duration even though they span two accounting years. Because of the short duration it is inappropriate to apportion the profits between the accounting periods. Profit should be recognized when the orders are completed. However, if a loss is foreseen it should be charged to the first accounting period.

(ii)

Works order number	488	517	518	519	Total
	£000	£000	£000	£000	
Valuation of work done	350	30	15	5	
Total sales value	450	135	18	9	
Direct costs incurred to date	(191)	(17)	(9)	(4)	
Overhead at 40% on labour	(42)	(4)	(2)	(0.8)	
Total costs to date	(233)	(21)	(11)	(4.8)	
Costs to complete, inclusive					
of overheads	(66)	(99)	–	–	
Total costs to complete	(299)	(120)			
Estimated contract profit	151	15			
Recognized profit	117(1)	nil (2)	nil (3)	nil (3)	117
Total costs incurred to date	233	21	11	4.8	
Less: included in cost of sales	233	–	–	–	
WIP	nil	21	11	4.8	36.8

Notes:

(1) $\dfrac{\text{Value of work certified (£350)}}{\text{Contract price (£450)}} \times$ Estimated profit from the contract (£151).

(2) No profit is taken since the contract is at an early stage of completion.

(3) Profit to be recognized on completion.

(iii) Attributing overheads to products on the basis of direct labour is justified if the majority of overhead resources consumed by products is caused by direct labour. In today's environment direct labour has diminished in importance and it is claimed that many overhead costs are caused by factors other than direct labour (such as the number of set-ups, number of orders placed, number of deliveries etc.). Using direct labour means that overheads allocated to orders will be reduced by reducing a diminishing labour content. However, the end result will be a minor reduction in direct labour costs. Those overheads that are not caused by direct labour will remain unchanged. Inaccurate product costs will also be reported.

(b) See the section on job and process costs in Chapter 2 and the introduction and Exhibit 6.2 in Chapter 6 for the answer to this question.

Process costing

Answers to Chapter 6

Question summary

6.1 to 6.5
Multiple choice questions.

6.6
An essay problem related to process costing.

6.7 to 6.9
Preparation of process accounts when there is no opening or closing WIP. Consequently, the problem of equivalent production does not arise. These questions require the preparation of abnormal loss and gain accounts.

6.10 and 6.11
Preparation of process accounts requiring the calculation of equivalent production and cost per equivalent unit using the weighted average basis. Neither problem includes any normal or abnormal losses.

6.12 to 6.16
Calculation of equivalent production and cost per equivalent unit using the weighted average basis. These questions include losses in process which are charged only to completed production. Questions 6.13, 6.15 and 6.16 involve losses in process which generate sales revenue. Questions 6.15 and 6.16 are the most difficult questions.

6.17
Similar to Questions 6.12 to 6.16 but with losses in process apportioned between work in progress and completed production.

6.18 and 6.19
Question 6.18 involves a loss in process detected on completion and 6.19 involves an abnormal gain.

6.20
Preparation of process accounts with normal and abnormal losses not requiring equivalent production calculations plus a description of weighted average and FIFO methods of stock valuation.

6.21 to 6.23
Calculation of cost per equivalent unit using the FIFO basis. All of these questions include losses in process. Question 6.22 is the most difficult question requiring the calculation of unit costs for both the weighted average and FIFO methods.

6.24
Cost control problem requiring the preparation of a performance report using equivalent production calculations.

Answer to question 6.6

(a) See section on job and process costs in Chapter 2 and the introduction to Chapter 6 for the answer to this problem.

(b) It would appear that a job costing system provides more accurate product costs because a separate cost is calculated for each job whereas with a process costing system the cost per unit is an average cost. On the other hand, a greater proportion of the costs are likely to be direct under process costing. With a job costing system, a large proportion of costs will be treated as overheads and the problem of apportioning and allocating overheads will result in inaccurate product costs. In this sense process costing might yield more accurate product costs. However, one problem with process costing is that there is a need to estimate the degree of completion of closing stocks of WIP in order to estimate equivalent units and cost per unit. If it is difficult to produce an accurate estimate of the degree of completion then the product costs will also be inaccurate. Therefore it depends on the circumstances – in some situations job costing product costs will be more accurate and in other situations process costing product costs may be more accurate.

Answer to question 6.7

(a) The question does not indicate the method of overhead recovery. It is assumed that overheads are to be absorbed using the direct wages percentage method.

Process A account

	Units	Price £	Amount £		Units	Price £	Amount £
Direct materials	6,000		12,000	Normal loss (scrap			
Direct materials added			5,000	account)	300	1.5	450
Direct wages			4,000	Process B	5,760	5.5	31,680
Direct expenses			800				
Production overhead			10,000				
(250% direct wages)			31,800				
Abnormal gain account	60	5.5	330				
	6,060		32,130		6,060		32,130

$$\text{Cost per unit} = \frac{\text{cost of production} - \text{scrap value of normal loss}}{\text{expected output}}$$

$$= \frac{£31,800 - £450}{5,700 \text{ units}} = £5.50$$

Process B account

	Units	Price £	Amount £		Units	Price £	Amount £
Process A	5,760	5.5	31,680	Normal loss (scrap			
Direct materials added			9,000	account)	576	2.0	1,152
Direct wages			6,000	Process C	5,100	12.0	61,200
Direct expenses			1,680	Abnormal loss	84	12.0	1,008
Production overhead							
(250% direct wages)			15,000				
	5,760		63,360		5,760		63,360

$$\text{Cost per unit} = \frac{£63,360 - £1,152}{5,760 - 576 \text{ units}} = £12$$

Process C account

	Units	Price £	Amount £		Units	Price £	Amount £
Process B	5,100		61,200	Normal loss (scrap			
Direct materials added			4,000	account)	255	4.0	1,020
Direct wages			2,000	Finished goods	4,370	16.0	69,920
Direct expenses			2,260	Process D	510	8.0	4,080
Production overhead							
(250% direct wages)			5,000				
			74,460				
Abnormal gain	35	16.0	560				
	5,135		75,020		5,135		75,020

$$\text{Cost per unit} = \frac{£74,460 - £1,020 - £4,080}{5,100 - 255 - 510 \text{ units}} = £16$$

Process D account (by-product)

	Units	Price £	Amount £		Units	Price £	Amount £
Process C	510		4,080	Normal loss (scrap			
Direct materials added			220	account)	51	2.0	102
Direct wages			200	Finished goods	450	11.0	4,950
Direct expenses			151	Abnormal loss	9	11.0	99
Production overhead							
(250% direct wages)			500				
	510		5,151		510		5,151

$$\text{Cost per unit} = \frac{£5,151 - £102}{510 - 51 \text{ units}} = £11$$

(b)

Abnormal gain account

	Units	Price £	Amount £		Units	Price £	Amount £
Normal loss account	60	1.5	90	Process A	60		330
Normal loss account	35	4.0	140	Process C	35		560
Profit and loss acount			660				
	95		890		95		890

Abnormal loss account

	Units	Price £	Amount £		Units	Price £	Amount £
Process B	84		1,008	Normal loss acount	84	2.0	168
Process D	9		99	Normal loss account	9	2.0	18
				Profit and loss account			921
	93		1,107		93		1,107

Normal loss account (income due)

	£		£
Process A normal loss	450	Abnormal gain account	90
Process B normal loss	1,152	Abnormal gain account	140
Process C normal loss	1,020		
Process D normal loss	102		
Abnormal loss account	168		
Abnormal loss account	18		

Answer to question 6.8

(a) See the sections on methods of apportioning joint costs to products and limitations of joint cost allocations for decision-making in Chapter 7 for the answer to this question.

(b)

Process 1

	Units	£		Units	£
Stock – material	3,000	15,000	Process 2	2,800	33,600
Components stock		1,000	Normal loss	300	600
Wages		4,000			
Expenses		10,000			
Production overhead		3,000			
		33,000			
Abnormal gain	100	1,200			
	3,100	34,200		3,100	34,200

$$\text{Cost per unit} = \frac{£33,000 - £600}{2,700} = £12$$

Process 2

	Units	£		Units	£
Process 1	2,800	33,600	Finished goods	2,600	59,800
Components stock		780	Normal loss	140	700
Wages		6,000	Abnormal loss	60	1,380
Expenses		14,000			
Production overhead		7,500			
	2,800	61,880		2,800	61,880

$$\text{Cost per unit} = \frac{£61,880 - £700}{2,600 \text{ units}} = £23$$

Finished goods

	£		£
Balance b/f	20,000	Cost of sales	56,800
Process 2	59,800	Balance	23,000
	79,800		79,800

Normal loss/scrap

	£		£
Process 1	600	Abnormal gain (process 1)	200
Process 2	700	Cash	1,100
	1,300		1,300

Abnormal loss

	£		£
Process 2	1,380	Cash	300
		Profit and loss account	1,080
	1,380		1,380

Abnormal gain

	£		£
Normal loss (100 × £2)	200	Process 1	1,200
Profit and loss account	1,000		
	1,200		1,200

Profit and loss account

	£		£
Abnormal loss	1,080	Abnormal gain	1,000

Answer to question 6.12

(a) *Statement of input and output:*

Input:	Units
Opening WIP	3,200
Current period input	24,800
	28,000

Output:	
Completed units	25,000
Closing WIP	2,500
Normal loss	500
	28,000

Statement of cost per unit:

Element of cost	Opening WIP £	Current cost £	Total cost £	Completed units	Normal loss	WIP equivalent units	Total equivalent units £	(a) Cost per unit £
Direct materials	14,000	96,000	110,000	25,000	500	2,500	28,000	3.9286
Conversion cost	19,500	177,375	196,875	25,000	500	1,250	26,750	7.3598
			306,875					11.2884

Value of work in progress:	£	£
Direct materials (2,500 units × £3.9286)	9,822	
Conversions cost (1,250 units × £7.3598)	9,200	19,022
Completed units (25,000 units at £11.2884)	282,210	
Add normal loss (500 × £11.2884)	5,643	287,853
		306,875

(b) Total cost of production transferred to finished stock = £287,853.

Note:
The question does not indicate at what stage in the process the normal loss occurs. It has been assumed that losses are detected at the completion stage. Consequently the cost of the normal loss is charged to completed production only.

Answer to question 6.13

(a) See Chapter 6 for the answer to this question.

(b) The question does not specify at what point in the production process the losses are detected. It is assumed that the losses are detected at the end of the process when production is fully complete. Therefore normal losses are not charged to WIP. The input to the process is 25,000 units and the output consists of 15,000 completed units, 6,000 WIP and a normal loss of 1,000 units (4% × 25,000). The balance of 3,000 units represents the abnormal loss.

Statement of equivalent production and calculation of cost per unit:

	Cost £	Comp units	Abnormal loss	Normal loss	Closing WIP	Total equiv. units	Cost per unit £	WIP £
Materials	62,000	15,000	3,000	1,000	6,000	25,000	2.48	14,880
Labour	44,000	15,000	3,000	1,000	4,000	23,000	1.913	7,652
Overhead	63,000	15,000	3,000	1,000	3,000	22,000	2.8636	8,592
	169,000						7.2566	31,124

Cost of completed units (15,000 × £7.2566)		108,850
Add normal loss (1,000 × £7.2566 − £2,000 scrap value)	5,256	114,106
Abnormal loss (3,000 × £7.2566)		21,770
		167,000

Process account

	Units	£		Units	£
Materials	25,000	62,000	Finished goods stock	15,000	114,106
Labour		44,000	Normal loss	1,000	2,000
Overhead		63,000	Abnormal loss	3,000	21,770
			WIP	6,000	31,124
	25,000	169,000		25,000	169,000

Abnormal loss account

	£		£
Process account	21,770	Profit and loss account	21,770

The question implies that there is no scrap value in respect of abnormal losses.

(c) See the section on normal and abnormal losses in Chapter 6 for the answer to this question. Normal losses are assumed to be uncontrollable losses that are inherent in the production process. Abnormal losses are avoidable and controllable and the firm should investigate abnormal losses, ascertain the reason for their ocurrence and take appropriate remedial action.

Answer to question 6.15

(a) *Production statement (units):*

Input:	Process 1	Process 2
Opening WIP	–	2,000
Input	15,000	10,000
	15,000	12,000
Output:		
Completed units	10,000	9,500
Normal loss (5%)	750	600
Closing WIP	4,400	1,800
Abnormal (gain)/loss (balance)	(150)	100
	15,000	12,000

It is assumed that losses are detected at the completion stage. Therefore normal losses are not charged to WIP.

Process 1 Statement of equivalent production and calculation of cost per unit:

	Cost £	Completed units	Normal loss	Abnormal gain	Closing WIP equiv. units	Total equiv units	Cost per unit £
Materials	26,740	10,000	750	(150)	3,520	14,120	1.8938
Labour	36,150	10,000	750	(150)	2,200	12,800	2.8242
Overhead	40,635	10,000	750	(150)	1,760	12,360	3.2876
	103,525						8.0056

	£	£
Value of closing WIP:		
Materials (3,520 units at £1.8938)	6,666	
Labour (2,200 units at £2.8242)	6,213	
Overhead (1,760 units at £3.2876)	5,786	
		18,665
Cost of completed units (10,000 × £8.0056)	80,056	
Add cost of normal loss (750 × £8.0056)	6,004	
		86,060
Cost allocated to abnormal gain (150 × £8.0056)		(1,200)
		103,525

Process 2 Statement of equivalent production and calculation of cost per unit:

	Opening WIP £	Current cost £	Total cost £	Comp. units	Normal loss	Abnormal loss	Closing WIP	Total equiv units	Cost per unit £
Previous process cost	17,000[a]	86,060[b]	103,060	9,500	600	100	1,800	12,000	8.5883
Labour	3,200	40,000	43,200	9,500	600	100	1,200	11,400	3.7895
Overhead	6,000	59,700	65,700	9,500	600	100	1,350	11,550	5.6883
	26,200		211,960						18.0661

	£	£	
Value of closing WIP:			
Previous process cost (1,800 × £8.5883)		15,459	
Labour (1,200 × £3.7895)		4,547	
Overhead (1,350 × £5.6883)		7,679	
			27,685
Completed units (9,500 × £18.0061)		171,628	
Add cost of normal loss (600 × £18.0661)	10,840		
Less sale proceeds of normal loss (600 × £8.0056)	4,803	6,037	177,665
Cost of abnormal loss (100 × £18.0661)			1,807
			207,157

Notes:
[a]Total opening WIP (£26,200) − labour (£3,200) − overheads (£6,000).
[b]Cost of completed production transferred from Process 1.

(i)

Process 1

	Units	£		Units	£
Material	15,000	26,740	Transfer to Process 2	10,000	86,060
Labour		36,150	Closing WIP	4,400	18,665
Overheads		40,635	Normal loss	750	
Abnormal gain	150	1,200			
	15,150	104,725		15,150	104,725

(ii)

Process 2

	Units	£		Units	£
Opening WIP	2,000	26,200	Finished units	9,500	177,665
Transfer from					
Process 1	10,000	86,060	WIP	1,800	27,685
Labour		40,000	Normal loss	600	4,803
Overheads		59,700	Abnormal loss	100	1,807
	12,000	211,960		12,000	211,960

(iii)

Normal loss account

	Units	£		Units	£
Process 2 account	600	4,803	Cash book	600	4,803

(iv)

Abnormal gain/(loss) account

	£		£
Process 2 account	1,807	Process 1 account	1,200
		Profit and loss account	607
	1,807		1,807

(b) See the introduction to Chapter 7 and the section on accounting for by-products in Chapter 7 for the answer to this question.

Answer to question 6.16

(a) See Chapter 6 for a description of each of the terms.

(b) See 'Normal and abnormal losses' in Chapter 6 for the answer to this question.

(c) *Workings*:

Process 1 abnormal gain = input (9,000) − (7,300 completed units + 1,800 normal loss)
= 100 units.

Process 2 abnormal loss = input (7,300) − (4,700 completed units + 2,000 WIP + 530 normal loss)
= 70 units.

It is assumed that the intention of the question is that normal loss is 10% of the input which reached the final inspection stage where the inspection occurs. Therefore normal loss is 530 units [10% × (7,300 input − 2,000 WIP)]. The cost per unit of output for process 1 is:

$$\frac{\text{cost of production} - \text{scrap value of normal loss}}{\text{expected output}}$$

$$= \frac{£14,964 + (2,450 \times £6) - (1,800 \times £1.20)}{(80\% \times 9,000)}$$

= £3.82

Process 1

	Units	£		Units	£
Materials	9,000	14,964	Completed units		
Conversion cost		14,700	(7,300 × 3.82)	7,300	27,886
Abnormal gain			Normal loss		
(100 × £3.82)	100	382	(1,800 × £1.20)	1,800	2,160
		30,046			30,046

Abnormal gain account

	£		£
Normal loss	120	Process 1	382
Profit and loss account	262		
	382		382

Normal loss (income due) account

	£		£
Process 1	2,160	Abnormal gain (100 × £1.20)	120
Process 1	753	Cash (balance)	2,793
	2,913		2,913

Process 2 account

	£		£
Process 1	27,886	Finished goods (W1)	24,456
Conversion cost	6,300	Normal loss (530 × £1.42)	753
		Abnormal loss (W1)	337
		Closing WIP (W1)	8,640
	34,186		34,186

Abnormal loss account

	£		£
Process 2	337	Cash (sale of £70 units at £1.42)	99
		Profit and loss account	238
	337		337

Working:

(W1) The cost per unit calculation for Process 2 is as follows:

	£	Completed units	Normal loss	Abnormal loss	WIP equivalent units	Total equivalent units	Cost per unit £	WIP value £
Previous process	27,886	4,700	530	70	2,000	7,300	3.82	7,640
Conversion cost	6,300	4,700	530	70	1,000	6,300	1.00	1,000
	34,186						4.82	8,640

	£	£
Completed units (4,700 × £4.82)		22,654
Share of normal loss (530 × £4.82)	2,554.60	
Less sale proceeds (530 × £1.42)	752.60	1,802
Cost of completed units		24,456
Abnormal loss (70 × £4.82)		337
WIP		8,640
		33,433

Note that the cost of the input (£34,186) less the sale proceeds of the normal loss equals the cost of the output. The normal loss of £1,802 ought to be apportioned between completed units and abnormal loss where this will have a significant impact on the value of completed units and abnormal loss. If this approach is adopted, the normal loss of £1,802 could be apportioned as follows:

Completed units [4,700/(4,700 + 70)] × £1,802 = £1,776
Abnormal loss [70/(4,700 + 70)] × £1,802 = £26

Given that the above adjustment will only have a minor effect on the process costs, there is little point in reflecting this apportionment in the process accounts.

Answer to question 6.19

In Chapter 6 (page 169) it was stated that if the normal loss was of significant value there are strong arguments for allocating this loss between the completed units and the abnormal loss (or abnormal gain). This is because the cost of the abnormal loss (gain) should be recorded at the cost per unit of normal output. The answer below adopts this approach but it is likely to be confusing for the student. For this question the students are likely to find the short-cut approach easier to understand. The answer using the short-cut approach is also shown below. Alternatively, lecturers may prefer to adopt the approach presented in the text and not allocate the normal loss between completed production and the abnormal gain.

Statement of cost per unit

	£	Completed units	Normal loss	Abnormal gain	Total equiv. units	Cost per unit £
Materials (1)	16,245	9,580	500	(80)	10,000	1.6245
Labour and overheads	28,596	9,580	300	(48)	9,832	2.9084
	44,841					4.5329

Note:
(1)   Period cost (£16,445) less normal scrap (500 × £0.40) = £16,245

Cost of normal loss to allocate to completed production and abnormal gain:

	£
Materials (500 units × £1.6245)	812.25
Labour and overhead (300 units × £2.9084)	872.52

Cost of normal loss allocated to completed production:

Materials (9,580/(9,580 + (−80)) × £812.25)	819.09
Labour and overhead (9,580/(9,580 + (−48)) × £872.52)	876.91
	1,696.00

Cost of completed production:

Completed units (9,580 × £4.5329)	43,425.18
Add share of normal loss	1,696.00
	45,121.18

Valuation of abnormal gain:

	£
Materials (80 × £1.6245)	129.96
Labour and overhead (48 × £2.9084)	139.60
Share of normal loss:	
Materials (80/9,580 + (−80)) × £812.25	6.84
Labour and overhead (48/9,580 + (−48)) × £872.52	4.39
	280.79

Statement of cost per unit using the short-cut method:

		Completed units	Abnormal gain	Total equiv. units	Cost per unit
	£				£
Materials	16,245	9,580	(80)	9,500	1.71
Labour and overhead	28,596	9,580	(48)	9,532	3.00
	44,841				4.71

		£
Cost of completed production (9,580 × £4.71)		45,121.80
Abnormal gain:		
Materials (80 units × £1.71)	136.80	
Labour and overhead (48 × £3)	144.00	280.80
Net cost		44,841.00

Process account

	£		£
Materials	16,445	Finished goods	45,121.80
Labour and overhead	28,596	Normal scrap	200.00
Abnormal gain	280.80		
	45,321.80		45,321.80

Normal loss (Income due)

	£		£
Process account	200	Abnormal gain (80 × 40p)	32
		Cash from scrap sold	
		(420 × 40p)	168
	200		200

Abnormal gain account

	£		£
Normal loss account	32	Process account	280.80
Profit and loss account	248.80		
	280.80		280.80

Answer to question 6.22

(a) (i) *Production statement:*

Input:	£
Opening WIP	21,700
Materials input	105,600
	127,300

Output:	
Completed units	92,400
Closing WIP	28,200
Normal loss (balance)	6,700
	127,300

Statement of equivalent production and calculation of cost per unit:

	Opening WIP £	Current cost £	Total cost £	Comp. units	Closing WIP equiv. units	Normal loss	Total equiv. units	Cost per unit £
Materials	56,420	276,672	333,092	92,400	28,200	6,700	127,300	2.6166
Conversion cost	30,597	226,195	256,792	92,400	14,100	–	106,500	2.4112
								5.0278

Losses are detected at the start of the process and therefore should be allocated between completed units and closing WIP. No conversion costs will be incurred in respect of the units lost. The cost of the normal loss is calculated as follows:

	£
Materials (6700 units × £2.6166)	17,531
Less scrap value of normal loss (6,700 × £0.45)	3,015
	14,516

The net cost of the normal loss relates to materials and the normal loss cost per unit of equivalent production is £0.1204 (£14,516/120,600). Therefore the cost per unit of equivalent production is:

	£
Materials (£2.6166 + £0.1204)	2.737
Conversion cost	2.4112
Total cost	5.1482

Alternatively, the short-cut method can be used when losses are apportioned between completed units and WIP. With this method normal losses are ignored in the calculation of equivalent units. The revised calculations are:

	Costs £	Completed units	WIP equiv. units	Total equiv. unit	Cost per unit £
Materials	330,077[a]	92,400	28,200	120,600	2.737
Conversion cost	256,792	92,400	14,100	106,500	2.4112
					5.1482

Note:
[a]£333,092 total cost less scrap value of normal loss (£3,015).

(a)   (ii)   *Production statement:*

	kg
Input:	
Opening WIP	21,700
Materials input	105,600
	127,300

Output:	
Completed units	92,400
Closing WIP	28,200
Normal loss (5% × 105,600)	5,280
Abnormal loss (balance)	1,420
	127,300

Statement of equivalent production and calculation of cost of completed production and WIP:

	Current cost £	Completed units less opening WIP requirements	Normal loss equiv. units	Abnormal loss equiv. units	Closing WIP equiv. units	Total equiv. units	Cost per unit £
Materials	276,672	70,700	5,280	1,420	28,200	105,600	2.62
Conversion cost	226,195	79,380	–	–	14,100	93,480	2.4197
							5.0397

The cost of the normal loss is calculated as follows:

	£
Materials (5,280 units × £2.62)	13,834
Less scrap value of normal loss (5,280 kg × £0.45)	2,376
	11,458

The cost of the normal loss is allocated in the ratio of equivalent production for materials between completed units, abnormal loss and closing WIP as follows:

	£
Completed units (70,700/100,320 × £11,458)	8,075
Abnormal loss (1,420/100,320 × £11,458)	162
Closing WIP (28,200/100,320 × £11,458)	3,221
	11,458

	£	£
Cost per equivalent unit of normal loss materials (£11,458/100,320)	0.1142	
Cost per equivalent unit of normal loss (excluding materials)	2.62	
Cost per unit (materials)	2.7342	
Cost per unit (conversion cost)	2.4197	
Total cost per unit	5.1539	

Cost of completed production:

Opening WIP (£56,420 + £30,597)	87,017	
Materials (70,700 × £2.62)	185,234	
Conversion cost (79,380 × £2.4197)	192,076	
Share of normal loss	8,075	
		472,402
Abnormal loss:		
Materials (1,420 × £2.62)	3,720	
Share of normal loss	162	
		3,882
Closing WIP:		
Materials (28,200 × £2.62)	73,884	
Conversion cost (14,100 × £2.4197)	34,118	
Share of normal loss	3,222	111,224
		587,508

(b)

Process account

Opening WIP:		Completed units	472,402
Materials	56,420	Abnormal loss	3,882
Conversion costs	30,597	Normal loss (sale	
		proceeds)	2,376
	87,017	Closing WIP	111,224
Input costs:			
Materials	276,672		
Conversion costs	226,195		
	589,884		589,884

(c) See introduction to Chapter 7 and 'Accounting for by-products' in Chapter 7 for the answer to this question.

Answer to question 6.24

(a)

Cost element	Opening WIP value £	Current cost £	Total cost £	Completed units	WIP equivalent units	Total equivalent units	Cost per unit £	WIP value £
Direct								
materials	17,400	162,600	180,000	8,200	800	9,000	20	16,000
Conversion	10,000	173,920	183,920	8,200	160	8,360	22	3,520
			363,920				42	19,520

Completed units 8,200 × £42 = 344,400

Total cost 363,920

Process account

	Units	£		Units	£
Opening WIP	1,000	27,400	Process B	8,200	344,400
Materials	8,000	162,600	Closing WIP c/d	800	19,520
Conversion cost		173,920			
		363,920			363,920

(b) *Calculation of equivalent production produced during current period:*

	Total equivalent units	Opening WIP equivalent units	Equivalent units produced during period
Materials	9,000	1,000	8,000
Conversion cost	8,360	400	7,960

Performance report:

	Standard cost £	Actual cost £	Difference £
Materials	160,000 (8,000 × £20)	162,600	2600 A
Conversion cost	183,080 (7,960 × £23)	173,920	9160 F
			6560 F

Joint product and by-product costing

Answers to Chapter 7

Question summary

Answer to question 7.2

(a) See Chapter 7 for the answer to this question.

(b) The answer should stress that joint cost apportionment should not be used for decision-making purposes. The sole purpose of joint cost apportionments is to value closing stock at the end of each accounting period in order to determine profit. If all production for the period were sold, the problem of joint cost apportionment would not exist. The two main methods of apportioning joint costs are the physical measures method and the sales value method. The sales value method is recommended. For an explanation of why this method is recommended see Chapter 7.

(c) See the section on opening and closing work in progress in Chapter 6 for the answer to this question.

Answer to question 7.3

(a) See Chapter 7 for the answer to this question.

(b) (i) It is rational to undertake a common process if the total revenue from the sale of the products from the joint process exceeds the joint costs plus further processing costs of those products which are further processed. Consider the following example.

A joint process costs £600, and joint products A, B and C emerge. The further processing costs and sales revenue from the finished products are as follows:

Product	Additional finishing costs £	Sales revenue from finished product £
A	300	600
B	400	800
C	500	1,000
	1,200	2,400

In the above example total revenue (£2,400) is greater than joint costs (£600) plus the additional costs of processing (£1,200). Therefore it is rational to undertake the joint process.

(ii) It is rational to 'finish off' each of the products from the joint process if the additional revenues from further processing exceed the additional costs of further processing. For an illustration of this statement see Example 7.1 in Chapter 7.

Answer to question 7.4

For the answer to this question see the sectons on methods of apportioning joint costs to products and limitations of joint cost allocations for decision-making in Chapter 7.

Answer to question 7.6

(a) Joint products and by-products arise in situations where the production of one product makes inevitable the production of other products. When a group of individual products is simultaneously produced, and each product has a significant relative sales value, the outputs are usually called joint products. Those products that are part of the simultaneous process and that have a *minor* sales value when compared to the joint products are called by-products.

Because by-products are of relatively *minor* sales value their net revenues are deducted from the joint processing costs before they are allocated to the joint products.

(b) Costs to apportion to joint products:
Joint process costs (£272,926) − Revenues from by-product C (2,770 × £0.80)
= £270,710

Market value of output:

		£
Joint product A (16,000 kg × £6.10) =		97,600
Joint product B (53,200 kg × £7.50) =		399,000
		496,600

Apportionment of joint costs:

Product A (£97,600/£496,600 × £270,710) =	£53,204
Product B (£399,000/£496,600 × £270,710) =	£217,506
	£270,710

Cost per kg:
Product A = £53,204/16,000   = £3.325
Product B = £217,506/53,200 = £4.088

(c)   Production costs:

	£
Material P: 3,220 kg at £5 per kg =	16,100
Material T: 6,440 kg at £1.60 per kg =	10,304
9,660	26,404
Conversion costs	23,796
	50,200

Analysis of output:

	kg
Completed production	9,130
Normal loss (5% × 9,660)	483
Abnormal loss (Balance)	47
Total input	9,660

$$\text{Cost per kg} = \frac{\text{Cost of production (£50,200)}}{\text{Expected output (9,660 kg} - \text{483 kg)}} = £5.47$$

Process Account

	Units	£		Units	£
Materials	9,660	26,404	Normal Loss	483	–
Conversion cost		23,796	Abnormal Loss (1)	47	257
			Output (2)	9,130	49,943
		50,200			50,200

Notes:
(1)   47 kg × £5.47 = £257
(2)   9,130 kg × £5.47 = £49,943

Answer to question 7.9

(a)   *Statement of input and output (litres):*

Input		Output	
Opening WIP	5,000	Joint product X	30,000
Transferred from process 1	65,000	Joint product Y	25,000
		By-product Z	7,000
	70,000	Normal loss (5% × 65,000)	3,250
		Closing WIP	6,000
			71,250
		Difference = Abnormal gain	(1,250)
			70,000

In Chapter 7 it was pointed out that by-products should not be charged with any portion of the joint costs that are incurred before the split-off point. Therefore the completed production for calculating the cost per unit of the joint process consists of 55,000 litres for X and Y and excludes the output of the by-product. It was also pointed out in Chapter 7 that by-product net revenues (the sales revenue of the by-product less the additional further processing costs after split-off point) should be deducted from the cost of the joint production process.

In order to simplify the answer the short-cut method is used. Also note that the opening WIP value of £60,000 is not analysed by the elements of cost. The question can therefore only be answered using the FIFO method. It is assumed that losses and gains consist of fully complete units.

Statement of cost per unit:

Cost element	Current period cost £	Completed units less opening WIP equivalent units	Abnormal gain	Closing WIP equivalent units	Current total equivalent units	Cost per unit £
Previous process cost[1]	547,500	50,000	(1,250)	6,000	54,750	10.00
Conversion cost	221,400	53,000	(1,250)	3,600	55,350	4.00
	768,900					14.00

	£	£
Completed production:		
Opening WIP	60,000	
Previous process cost (50,000 × £10)	500,000	
Conversion cost (53,000 × £4)	212,000	772,000
Closing WIP		
Previous process cost (6,000 × £10)	60,000	
Conversion cost (3,600 × £4)	14,400	74,400
Abnormal gain (1,250 × £14)		(17,500)
		828,900

Note:

(1) Previous process cost = £578,500 − by-product net revenue (7,000 × £3.50) − Scrap value of normal loss (3,250 × £2).

It is assumed that joint costs are to be allocated on the basis of net realisable value at split-off point:

	£
Paint X (30,000 × (£15 − £0.50) =	435,000
Paint Y (25,000 × (£18 − £2)) =	400,000
	835,000

Allocated to Paint X (£435/£835 × £772,000) = £402,180
Allocated to Paint Y (£400/£835 × £772,000) = £369,820

Process 2 account, October 1997

	Litres	£		Litres	£
Opening WIP	5,000	60,000	Normal loss	3,250	6,500
Process 1	65,000	578,500	Paint X	30,000	402,180
Direct labour		101,400	Paint Y	25,000	369,820
Variable overhead		80,000	By-product Z	7,000	24,500
Fixed overhead		40,000	Closing WIP	6,000	74,400
Abnormal gain	1,250	17,500			
	71,250	877,400		71,250	877,400

(b) To help you understand the answer the normal loss account is also shown below:

Normal Loss (Income due)

	£		£
Process 2 Account	6,500	Abnormal gain (1,250 × £2)	2,500
		Cash from scrap sold	
		(2,000 × £2)	4,000
	6,500		6,500

Abnormal Gain Account:

	£		£
Normal Loss account	2,500	Process 2 Account	17,500
Profit and loss account	15,000		
	17,500		17,500

(c) See the section on methods of apportioning joint costs to joint products for the answer to this question.

Answer to question 7.11

(a)

Product	Output	Unit price	Sales value	%	Allocated
	£	£		£	
A	8,000	5	40,000	10.3	20,600
B	20,000	5	100,000	25.6	51,200
C	25,000	10	250,000	64.1	128,200
			390,000	100	200,000

(b)

	Modification costs	Input	Total modification cost
	£		£
Max A	8	8,000	64,000
Max B	12	20,000	240,000
Max C	16	25,000	400,000

	Revenue	Output	Total extra revenue
	£		£
Max A	144,000	7,200	104,000
Max B	414,000	18,000	314,000
Max C	495,000	22,500	245,000

	Contribution from modification
Max A	40,000
Max B	74,000
Max C	(155,000)

Max A and Max B should be produced.

(c)

	Contribution	Output tonnes	Labour hours	Contribution per labour hour
	£			£
Max A	40,000	7,200	8,000	5.0
Max B	74,000	18,000	30,000	2.5

Production should be concentrated on Max A since this produces the greatest benefit per hour of the scarce resource. Max B should not be produced.

Answer to question 7.13

(a)

Product	Sales value £000	Costs beyond split-off point £000	Net sales value £000	Proportion of total %	Joint costs apportioned £000
Q	768	160	608	62.30	456
R	232	128	104	10.65	78
S	32	–	32	3.28	24
T	240	8	232	23.77	174
	1,272	296	976		732

Budgeted product profitability statement:

	Q £000	R £000	S £000	T £000	Total £000
Sales	768	232	32	240	1272
Joint process costs	(456)	(78)	(24)	(174)	(732)
Further processing costs	(160)	(128)		(8)	(296)
Profit	152	26	8	58	244

(b)

Sales	512	144	32	180	868
Joint process costs	(456)	(78)	(24)	(174)	(732)
Profit	56	66	8	6	136

(c)

	Q £000	R £000	T £000
Incremental revenue from further processing	256 (768 − 512)	88 (232 − 144)	60 (240 − 180)
Additional processing costs	160	128	8
Incremental net revenue	96	(40)	52

Product R should be sold at split-off point, since the additional further processing costs exceed the incremental revenues. The overall profit will therefore rise from £244,000 to £284,000.

Answer to question 7.14

(a)

Process 1 account

	Litres	CPU £	£		Litres	CPU £	£
Direct materials	80,000	1.25	100,000	Normal loss	8,000	0.50	4,000
Direct wages			48,000	Output A	22,000	2.50	55,000
Production overhead			36,000	B	20,000	2.50	50,000
(75% of direct				C	10,000	2.50	25,000
wages)				D	18,000	2.50	45,000
				Abnormal			
				loss	2,000	2.50	5,000
	80,000		184,000		80,000		184,000

$$\text{Cost per unit} = \frac{£184,000 - £4,000}{72,000 \text{ litres}} = £2.50 \text{ per litre}$$

Profit and loss statement:

	A	B	C	D	Total
Sales (litres)	22,000	20,000	10,000	18,000	
Selling price per litre (£)	4	3	2	5	
Sales (£000)	88	60	20	90	
Joint cost apportionment from Process A (£000)	(55)	(50)	(25)	(45)	
Post separation costs: direct wages + overhead (£000)	(21)	(14)	(7)	(28)	
Profit/(loss)	12	(4)	(12)	17	13

Note that the profit will be reduced by the £5,000 abnormal loss.

(b) Profit from the present output can be maximized by further processing only those products whose incremental revenues exceed the incremental costs.

	A	B	C	D	Total
Incremental revenue per litre (£)	1.50	0.20	0.80	2.00	
Output (litres)	22,000	20,000	10,000	18,000	
Incremental revenue (£000)	33	4	8	36	
Incremental costs of further processing (£000)	(21)	(14)	(7)	(28)	
Contribution to joint costs	12	(10)	1	8	11

Product B should not be subject to further processing, since it yields £10,000 negative contribution. It is assumed that overheads and direct labour are avoidable costs. If the overheads are fixed costs (i.e. not avoidable costs) and the direct wages are avoidable costs, it is still not worthwhile further processing product B.

Revised profit statement:

	A	B	C	D	Total
Sales (£000)	88	56	20	90	
Post separation costs (£000)	21	–	7	28	
Contribution to joint costs (£000)	67	56	13	62	198
Less joint costs (£000)					175
Revised profit (£000)					23

Note the above profit will be reduced by the £5,000 abnormal loss.

(c)   Product B should not be processed beyond process 1, and the abnormal loss should be investigated. Product C makes a loss, but an alternative apportionment method (e.g. the sales value method) might indicate that it makes a profit. The important point to note is that the process as a whole yields a profit. If product C were abandoned, the common and unavoidable joint costs would still continue, but the company would lose the sales revenue of £20,000.

Absorption costing and variable costing

Answers to Chapter 8

Question summary

8.1 and 8.2
Multiple choice questions.

8.3 and 8.4
Discussion questions relating to Chapter 8.

8.4 to 8.15
Preparation of variable costing and absorption costing profit statements and computation of stock valuations. Questions 8.7, 8.9, 8.11, 8.13 and 8.14 require the reconciliation of absorption costing and variable costing profits. Question 8.12 also requires a statement of equivalent production in order to calculate product costs. The most difficult questions are 8.13 to 8.15. Question 8.15 involves the reapportionment of service department costs and the calculation of overhead rates prior to the preparation of profit statements. Question 8.14 requires the preparation of absorption and variable costing statements using both FIFO and average costing methods.

Answer to question 8.3

See Chapter 8 for the answer to this question.

Answer to question 8.4

See Chapter 8 for the answer to this question.

Answer to question 8.5

(a) The question does not specify the predetermined annual activity. It is assumed that fixed overheads are to be recovered on the basis of monthly activity.

Fixed overhead rate = £75,000 fixed overheads/monthly direct wages (£75,000)
$$= 100\% \text{ of direct wages}$$

Fixed overhead rate per unit of output = £3 direct labour × 100% = £3
Variable cost per unit of output   = £10
Absorption cost per unit of output   = £13

Absorption costing profit statements:

	January £		February £	
Opening stock	–		91,000	(7,000 × £13)
Production cost	325,000	(25,000 × £13)	325,000	(25,000 × £13)
	325,000		416,000	
Less closing stock	91,000	(7,000 × £13)	–	
	234,000		416,000	
Sales	288,000	(18,000 × £46)	512,000	(32,000 × £16)
Profit	54,000		96,000	

Marginal costing profit statements:

	January £		February £	
Opening stock	–		70,000	(7,000 × £10)
Variable production cost	250,000	(25,000 × £10)	250,000	(25,000 × £10)
	250,000		320,000	
Less closing stock	70,000	(7,000 × £40)	–	
	180,000		320,000	
Add fixed overheads	75,000		75,000	
	255,000		395,000	
Sales	288,000		512,000	
Profit	33,000		117,000	

(b)   Stock valuation (see (a)) are £91,000 (absorption cost) and £70,000 (marginal cost).

(c)   The total profits over the two periods are identical (£150,000) for both methods because production equals sales over this period. In January, profits are higher with the absorption costing method because production exceeds sales and some of the fixed overheads are included in the closing stock valuation. In February, the situation is reversed and sales exceed production. Therefore opening stock is greater than the closing stock and the fixed overheads charged as an expense will exceed the fixed overheads incurred for the period. In contrast, the marginal costing method treats the fixed overhead incurred during the period as a period cost. For a more detailed explanation of the difference in reported profits see the section on variable costing and absorption costing: a comparison of their impact on profit in Chapter 8.

(d)   For the answer to this question see the section on some arguments in support of absorption costing in Chapter 8.

(e)   This question refers to the advantages of the decision-relevant cost approach described in Chapter 10. Situations where the marginal costing approach aids decision-making (see Chapter 10 for illustrations) include:
    (i)   make-or-buy decisions;

Answer to question 8.7

(a)   (i)   *Marginal costing:*

		March £			April £
Sales: 1,500 at £35		52,500			
3,000 at £35					105,000
Less Variable cost of sales					
Opening stock				7,500	
Variable manufacturing					
cost (2,000 × £15)	30,000		(3,200 × £15)	48,000	
				55,500	
Less Closing stock (500 × £15)	7,500		(700 × £15)	10,500	
	22,500			45,000	
Variable selling, distribution					
and administration					
15% of sales	7,875			15,750	
		30,375			60,750
Contribution		22,125			44,250
Less Fixed costs:					
Production (W1)	15,000			15,000	
Selling, distribution					
and administration	10,000			10.000	
		25,000			25,000
Profit/(loss)		£(2,875)			£19,250

(ii)   *Absorption costing:*

		March £			April £
Sales: 1,500 at £35		52,500			
3,000 at £35					105,000
Less Cost of sales:					
Opening stock	–			10,000	
Production cost (2,000 × £20)	40,000		(3,200 × £20)	64,000	
				74,000	
Less Closing stock (500 × £20)	10,000		(700 × £20)	14,000	
	30,000			60,000	
Fixed production overhead					
Under-/(over-) absorbed (W2)	5,000			(1,000)	
Production cost of sales		35,000			59,000
Gross profit		17,500			£46,000

Less	Variable selling distribution and administration:				
	15% of sales	7,875		15,750	
	Fixed selling, distribution and administration	10,000		10,000	
			17,875		25,750
(Loss)/profit			(375)		20,250

Workings:

W1 Monthly fixed overheads = (36,000 units ÷ 12 months) × £5 = £15,000

W2 In March the output is 1,000 units less than the normal monthly activity of 3,000 units resulting in an under recovery of £5,000. In April output is 200 units in excess of normal activity resulting in an over recovery of £1,000.

(b) *Reconciliation profit statement:*

	March £		April £	
Marginal costing profit/(loss)	(2,875)		19,250	
Fixed overhead included in increase in stocks using absorption costing and not charged as an expense in current period	2,500	(500 × £5)	1,000	(200 × £5)
Absorption costing profit (loss)	(375)		20,250	

In March, stocks have increased by 500 units. Absorption costing charges fixed overheads to products. Consequently, £2,500 (500 × £5) fixed overhead is included in the stock valuation and not charged as an expense in March.

The fixed overheads incurred (£15,000) are charged as a period cost with the marginal costing system. In April, stocks increase by 200 units and therefore the increase in the stock valuation includes £1,000 fixed overheads. Thus £14,000 production fixed overheads are charged as an expense with the absorption costing system.

(c) The answer should indicate that SSAP 9 requires that absorption costing should be used for external reporting. For internal reporting, marginal costing (that is, variable costing) is normally favoured. (See Chapter 8 for an explanation of why variable costing is preferable.)

Answer to question 8.8

(a) *Calculation of unit costs and selling price:*

	£
Variable production cost	16
Fixed production cost (£800,000/160,000)	5
Total production cost	21
Variable selling, distribution and administration costs	8
Fixed selling, distribution and administration costs	7.50
Total cost	36.50
Selling price	40

(i) *Marginal costing statement:*

	£000
Variable production cost (55,000 × £16)	880
Less closing stock (15,000 × £16)	240
Variable cost of goods sold	640
Fixed manufacturing cost (£800,000/4 quarters)	200
Total production cost	840
Variable non-manufacturing costs (40,000 × £8)	320
Fixed non-manufacturing costs (£1,200/4 quarters)	300
Total cost	1,460
Sales (40,000 × £40)	1,600
Profit	140

(ii) *Absorption costing statement:*

	£000
Full production cost (55,000 × £21)	1,155
Less closing stock (15,000 × £21)	315
Cost of goods sold	840
Less over absorption of fixed overheads (15,000 × £5)	75
Total production cost	765
Variable non-manufacturing costs	320
Fixed non-manufacturing costs	300
Total cost	1,385
Sales	1,600
Profit	215

(b) For the answer to this question see the section on variable costing and absorption costing: a comparison of their impact on profit in Chapter 8. In particular, the answer should draw attention to the 15,000 units increase in stocks in part (a). With an absorption costing system, £75,000 fixed overhead (15,000 units × £5) is included in the closing stock valuation and deferred as an expense until the next accounting period. In contrast, with the marginal costing system the full amount of production fixed overheads is charged as an expense in the current accounting period. Therefore profits are £75,000 higher with the absorption costing system. SSAP9 requires that all non-manufacturing costs are treated as period costs. Hence both systems treat non-manufacturing costs as period costs.

(c)
Budgeted contribution per unit	£50
Budgeted total contribution (profit plus fixed costs)	£1,200,000
Budgeted sales volume	£24,000 (£1,200,000/£50)

Strategy 1:
24,000 (1.10) sales volume × unit contribution (£50 − [0.05 × £80])
= £1,214,400 total contribution

Strategy 2:
24,000 (1.20) sales volume × unit contribution (£50 − [0.075 × £80])
= £1,267,200 total contribution

Strategy 3:
24,000 (1.25) sales volume × unit contribution (£50 − [0.10 × £80])
= £1,260,000 total contribution

The above information suggests that strategy 2 should be chosen since it yields a contribution of £67,200 in excess of the budgeted contribution.

Answer to question 8.10

(a)   (i) *Absorption costing:*

	September £000		October £000	
Opening stock	–		730.24	(28,000 × £26.08)
Production cost	2,999.20	(115,000 × £26.08)	2,034.24	(78,000 × £26.08)
Less closing stock	730.24	(28,000 × £26.08)	130.40	(5000 × £26.08)
	2,268.96		2,634.08	
Under/(over) absorption (*W1*)	(208.80)		45.44	
	2,060.16		2,679.52	
Non-manufacturing overheads	200.00		200.00	
Total cost	2,260.16		2,879.52	
Sales	2,784.00	(87,000 × £32)	3,232.00	(101,000 × £32)
Net profit	523.84		352.48	

Working:

W1 100% capacity production = 1,008,000/0.7 = 1,444,000 gross per annum
                                          =   120,000 gross per month

	September	October
Production (units)	115,000	78,000
Capacity	96%	65%
Fixed costs (£)	656,000	632,000
Fixed overhead absorbed (£):		
115,000 × £7.52	864,800	–
78,000 × £7.52	–	586,560
Under/(over) absorption (£)	(208,800)	45,440

(ii) *Marginal costing:*

	September £000		October £000	
Opening stock	–		519.68	(28,000 × £18.56)
Production cost	2,134.40	(115,000 × £18.56)	1,447.68	(78,000 × £18.56)
Less closing stock	519.68	(28,000 × £18.56)	92.80	(5,000 × £18.56)
	1,614.72		1,874.56	
Fixed production costs	656.00		632.00	
Non-manufacturing overheads	200.00		200.00	
	2,470.72		2,706.56	
Sales	2,784.00	(87,000 × £32)	3,232.00	(101,000 × £32)
Net profit	313.28		525.44	

(b) For cost control purposes flexible budgets should be used and costs should be separated into their fixed and flexible elements. Using absorption costing for stock valuation and profit measurement purposes therefore does not preclude the analysis of fixed and variable costs for cost control purposes.

Marginal costing does not eliminate any distortion of interim profits where seasonal fluctuations in sales occur and production is at a fairly constant level. Marginal costing exerts a smoothing effect only when sales are relatively stable and production fluctuates from period to period.

The adoption of a relevant costing/variable costing approach for decision-making is not dependent upon stocks being valued on an absorption costing basis. The statement is confusing decision-making applications with cost information required for stock valuation and profit measurement purposes. However, break-even analysis is based on the assumption that profits are measured on a marginal costing basis, and consequently marginal costing is preferable for profit planning purposes.

Answer to question 8.15

(a) *Calculation of fixed manufacturing overhead rate (£000):*

	Prodn dept 1	Prodn dept 2	Service dept	General factory	Total
Allocated	380.0	465.0	265	230	1,340
Allocation of general factory	92.0 (40%)	115.0 (50%)	23 (10%)	(230)	
Share of service department:			288		
Labour related costs (60%)	76.8 (8/18)	96.0 (10/18)	(172.8)		
Machine related costs (40%)	57.6	57.6	(115.2)		
	606.4	733.6			1,340
Units of output (000)	120	120			
Overhead rate per unit (£)	5.0533	6.1133			

Calculation of total manufacturing cost per unit:

	£
Direct materials	7.00
Direct labour	5.50
Variable overhead	2.00
Fixed overhead: department 1	5.0533
department 2	6.1133
Manufacturing cost	25.6666

Absorption costing profit statement:

	£000
Production cost (116,000 × £25.666)	2,977.33
Less closing stocks (2,000 × £25.6666)	51.33
Cost of sales	2,926.00
Under absorption of overhead:	
Department 1 (£20,000 + (4,000 × £5.0533))	40.21
Department 2 (4,000 units × £6.1133)	24.45
Non-manufacturing costs	875.00
Total cost	3,865.66
Sales (114,000 × £36)	4,104.00
Net profit	238.34

Note that the under recovery of fixed overheads consists of £20,000 arising from actual overheads exceeding estimated overheads plus 4,000 times the fixed overhead rate because actual volume was 4,000 units less than estimated volume.

(b) *Marginal costing profit statement:*

	£000
Variable production cost (116,000 × £14.50)	1,682
Less closing stocks (2,000 × £14.50)	29
	1,653
Fixed manufacturing overhead (1,340 + 20)	1,360
Non-manufacturing overhead	875
	3,888
Sales	4,104
Net profit	216

(c) See the section on variable costing and absorption costing: a comparison of their impact on profit in Chapter 8 for the answer to this question. The answer should also explain why the profits calculated on an absorption costing basis in (a) exceed the variable costing profit computation in (b) by £22,340 (£238,340 − £216,000). This is because stocks have increased by 2,000 units and with the absorption costing profit computation fixed manufacturing overheads of approximately £22,340 (2,000 units × £11.166 fixed overhead rate) are included in the closing stock valuation. Therefore £22,340 of the fixed overheads is incurred as an expense in the following period. The total fixed manufacturing overhead charged as an expense against the current period is £1,337,660 ((116,000 × £11.166) − (2,000 × £11.166) + £64,660 under absorption). With the variable costing system all of the fixed overheads incurred during the period of £1,360,000 is charged as an expense against the current accounting period. The difference between the fixed overheads charged as an expense (£1,337,660 − £1,360,000) accounts for the difference in the profit computation.

Cost–volume–profit analysis

Answers to Chapter 9

Question summary

9.1 to 9.7
Multiple choice questions.

9.8 to 9.10
Discussion question on cost–volume–profit (CVP) analysis.

9.11 to 9.17
Construction of breakeven or profit-volume graphs. Question 9.12 requires the calculation of variable costs using the high-low method of analysing fixed and variable costs. Question 9.15 includes a change in the sales mix and Question 9.16 requires the preparation of a multi-product profit-volume graph. Question 9.17 includes an increase in fixed costs.

9.18 to 9.24
These questions consist of a variety of CVP analysis problems using a non-graphical approach. Question 9.22 also requires the separation of fixed and variable costs using the high-low method.

9.25
A simple problem which can be used to illustrate the product mix assumptions of CVP analysis.

9.26 and 9.27
More difficult questions requiring the calculation of breakeven points based on different sales mix assumptions. Question 9.27 also involves a product abandonment decision.

9.28 to 9.34
More demanding CVP analysis problems using a non-graphical approach. These problems place a greater emphasis on decision-making aspects. Question 9.30 also involves key factor decision-making.

Answer to question 9.8

(a) The selling price is in excess of the variable cost per unit, thus providing a contribution towards fixed costs and profit. At point (A) sales are insufficient to generate a contribution to cover the fixed costs (difference between total cost and variable cost lines in the diagram). Consequently a loss occurs. Beyond the break-even point sales volume is sufficient to provide a contribution to cover fixed costs, and a profit is earned. At point (B) the increase in volume is sufficient to generate a contribution to cover fixed costs and provide a profit equal to the difference (represented by the dashed line) between the total revenue and cost line.

(b) See Chapter 9 for the answer to this question.

Answer to question 9.9

The comparisons of CVP models represented in management accounting and economic theory are presented in the first half of Chapter 9. Additional points include the following:

(i) Both models are concerned with explaining the relationship between changes in costs and revenues and changes in output. Both are simplifications of cost and revenue functions because variables other than output affect costs and revenues.

(ii) The value of both models is reduced when arbitrary cost allocation methods are used to apportion joint costs to products or divisions.

(iii) The economic model indicates two break-even points whereas the management accounting model indicates one break-even point.

(iv) Both models are based on single value estimates of total costs and revenues. It is possible to incorporate uncertainty into the analysis using probability statistics.

(v) The model based on economic theory provides a theoretical presentation of the relationship between costs, revenues and output. The model is intended to provide an insight into complex inter-relationships. The management accounting model should be seen as a practical decision-making tool which provides a useful approximation for decision-making purposes if certain conditions apply (e.g. relevant range assumption).

Answer to question 9.10

(a) See the section on cost–volume–profit analysis assumptions in Chapter 9 for the answer to this question.

(b) Examples of the circumstances where the underlying assumptions are violated include:

(i) *Variable cost per unit remaining constant over the entire range*: This assumption is violated where quantity discounts can be obtained from the purchase of larger quantities. Consequently the variable cost per unit will not be constant for all output levels. However, over a restricted range, or several restricted ranges, a linear relationship or a series of linear relationships may provide a reasonable approximation of the true cost function.

(ii) *Selling price is constant per unit*: In order to increase sales volume, the selling price might be reduced. Therefore selling price will not be a linear function of volume. A series of linear relationships may provide a reasonable approximation of the true revenue function.

(iii) *The sales mix is known*: It is unlikely that the planned sales mix will be equal to the actual sales mix. To incorporate the possibility that the actual sales mix may differ from the planned sales mix, a range of total cost and revenue curves should be prepared corresponding to each possible sales mix. This will give a range of break-even points and profit/losses for possible mixes of sales.

Answer to question 9.14

(a) (i) Variable cost per unit = £19 (£171,000/9,000 units)

BEP   = Fixed costs(£78,000)/
                  Contribution per unit (£13)
              = 6,000 units

BEP (sales value) = 6,000 units × £32 = £192,000

(ii) See Fig. 9.14 for the answer to this question.

(iii) From the graph in Fig. 9.14 it can be seen that at full capacity the company could be expected to produce a profit of £78,000.

(b) *Proposal 1:*

	£
Total contribution = (90% × 12,000 units × £9) =	97,200
Less fixed overhead =	78,000
Profit	19,200

Proposal 2:

	£
Total contribution = (12,000 units × £8.20) =	98,400
Less fixed overhead (£78,000 + £5,000) =	83,000
Profit	15,400

Based on the above information management ought to adopt the original budget plan as this yields the largest profit.

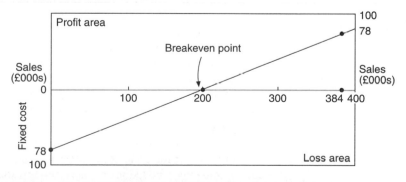

Figure 9.14 Answer to Problem 9.14(a) (ii): profit–volume graph

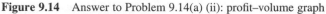

(c) Contribution = 12,0000 units × £13 £
                                    = 156,000
    Less fixed costs (£78,000 + £15,000)   = 93,000
    Profit   63,000

This proposal yields the largest profit and therefore should be accepted. However, there is a risk that the estimated sales demand will not be obtained and this could result in a reduced profit since the £15,000 will be a committed cost irrespective of the outcome. Management would need some assurance that the market research company is reliable and has a good track record.

Answer to question 9.16

(a)

Product	Unit contribution	Sales volume (units)	Total contribution £000	Total sales revenue £000
J	6	10,000	60	200
K	32	10,000	320	400
L	(0.20)	50,000	(10)	200
M	3	20,000	60	200
		90,000	430	1,000

Average contribution = 43% of sales revenue

(b) and (c) The profit arising from the most profitable product (Product K) is drawn first on the profit–volume graph (see Fig. Q9.16). At £400,000 sales revenue a profit of £80,000 (£320,000 contribution − £240,000 fixed costs) is plotted on the graph. The profits arising from the remaining products are then entered on the graph. Since fixed costs have already been covered by Product K, the next product (Product J) will increase profits by £60,000 (i.e. total contribution of £60,000). The second point to be plotted is therefore cumulative sales of £600,000 and profits of £140,000. The addition of Product M results in cumulative profits of £200,000 (£140,000 + £60,000) and cumulative sales revenue of £800,000. Finally, the addition of product L reduces total profits to £190,000.

    The dashed line on the graph represents the average contribution per £1 of sales (43%) arising from the planned sales mix. The break-even point in sales value is £558,140 [fixed costs (£240,000)/contribution ratio (0.43)]. This is the point where the dashed line cuts the horizontal axis. At zero sales level a loss equal to the fixed costs will be incurred and at the maximum sales level profits will be £190,000 [(£1m × 0.43) − £240,000].

    Product K yields the largest contribution/sales ratio (80%) and Products J and M yield identical ratios. Product L has a negative contribution and discontinuation will result in profits increasing by £10,000.

(d) The contribution/sales ratio can be improved by:
  (i) increasing selling price;
  (ii) reducing unit variable costs by improving labour efficiency or obtaining cheaper materials from different suppliers;
  (iii) automating production and substituting variable costs with fixed costs.

Answer to question 9.17

(a) See the section on cost–volume–profit analysis assumptions in Chapter 9 for the answer to this question.

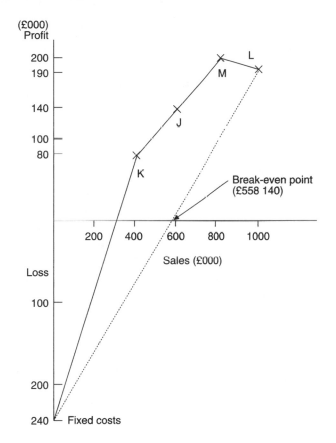

Figure 9.16

(b) (i) *Holiday resort cost and income statement:*

Guests in residence	Income p.a. £	Variable costs £	Contribution £	Fixed costs £	Surplus (deficit) £
6	18,000	7,740	10,260	16,000	(5,740)
7	21,000	9,030	11,970	16,000	(4,030)
8	24,000	10,320	13,680	16,000	(2,320)
9	27,000	11,610	15,390	16,000	(610)
10	30,000	12,900	17,100	16,000	1,100
11	33,000	14,190	18,810	22,000	(3,190)
12	36,000	15,480	20,520	22,000	(1,480)
13	39,000	16,770	22,230	22,000	230
14	42,000	18,060	23,940	22,000	1,940
15	45,000	19,350	25,650	22,000	3,650

There are two break-even points. If provision is made for between 6 and 10 guests, the first break-even point occurs just in excess of 9 guests per week (or 270 guests per annum). If provision is made for 11 or more guests per week, the break-even point changes to 13 guests per week.

(ii) The total costs for various activity levels are as follows:

Guests	Total costs
	£
6	23,740
10	28,900
11	36,190
15	41,350

The above costs are plotted on the break-even chart shown in Figure 9.17.

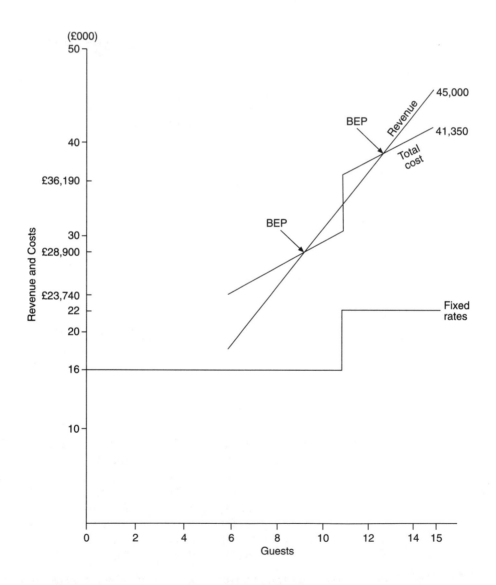

Figure Q9.17

COST–VOLUME–PROFIT ANALYSIS

Answer to question 9.18

(a) BEP = Fixed costs (£240,000)/contribution per unit (£15)
    = 16,000 pairs

		£
(b)	Contribution (20,000 × £15) =	300,000
	Less fixed costs	240,000
		60,000

(c)
Required total contribution		£250,000
Revised unit contribution		£13
Required sales		19,231 pairs (£250,000/£13)

(d) $$BEP = \frac{\text{Fixed cost (£24,000)} + £20,000}{\text{Unit contribution (£19.80)}}$$

= 13,131 pairs

Answer to question 9.20

(a)

Products	X	Y	Z
	£	£	£
Selling price	15	25	10
Variable costs:			
Materials	(3)	(5)	(4)
Labour	(6)	(8)	(5.50)
Overhead	(1)	(2)	(1.50)
Contribution	5	10	(1)

Note:

	X	Y	Z
	£	£	£
(1) Overhead cost per unit	2.25	4.50	2.75
Less fixed overhead unit cost			
(machine time × £5)	1.25	2.50	1.25
	1.00	2.00	1.50

(b)

	X	Y	Z	Total
				£
Contribution per unit	£5	£10	(£1)	
Units sold	100,000	80,000	120,000	
Total contribution	£500,000	£800,000	(£120,000)	1,180,000
Less fixed costs (1)				825,000
Profit				355,000

Note:

		£
(1) Labour fixed costs		350,000
Fixed overheads (Product X = 100,000 × £1.25)		125,000
(Product Y = 80,000 × £2.50)		200,000
(Product Z = 120,000 × £1.25)		150,000
		825,000

(c) *Proposal 1:*

	£
Increase in variable overheads per unit	0.15
Decline in material cost	0.75
Increase in unit contribution	0.60
Increase in total contribution (120,000 × £0.60)	72,000
Reduction in fixed costs	75,000
Increase in profits	147,000

Total profits will increase by £147,000 from £355,000 to £502,000.

Proposal 2:
An increase in the selling price will increase contribution by £1 per unit and total contribution will increase by £120,000 (120,000 units × £1). Total profits will be £475,000 (£355,000 + £120,000).

Proposal 3:

	£
Savings in negative contribution (120,000 × £1)	120,000
Savings in fixed labour costs	90,000
	210,000
Less redundancy payments	50,000
Increase in profits	160,000

The revised profits will be £515,000 (£355,000 + £160,000).

(d) Proposal 3 should be adopted since this maximizes profits. Proposal 1 yields a lower contribution and may result in reduced quality. With Proposal 3 it is questionable whether the proposed sales will be achieved in view of the depressed state of the market.

Answer to question 9.22

(a) For the answer to this question you should refer to 'cost behaviour' within the sections on classification for decision-making and planning and classification for control in chapter 2.

(b)

	Output (units)	Total cost £
Lowest activity	11,500	102,476
Highest activity	14,000	113,201
	2,500	10,725

$$\text{Variable cost per unit of output} = \frac{\text{Difference in cost (£10,725)}}{\text{Difference in output (2,500 units)}}$$

$$= \text{£4.29 per unit}$$

The fixed cost can be estimated at any level of activity by subtracting the variable cost portion from the total cost. At an activity level of 11,500 units the total cost is £102,476 and the total variable cost is £49,335 (11,500 units × £4.29). The balance of £53,141 is assumed to represent the fixed costs.

(c) $\text{Break-even point} = \dfrac{\text{Fixed costs (£53,141)}}{\text{Contribution per unit (£10.60 − £4.29)}} = 8,422 \text{ units}$

Because the break-even point is outside the range of observations that were used to estimate the variable and fixed costs it is possible that estimates of cost behaviour may not be accurate. However, given that the lowest observed level of activity is significantly above the break-even point output level there is a very high probability that profits will be generated at all likely levels of activity.

Answer to question 9.26

(a) (i)

Product	P	E
Unit contribution	£5	£2
Weightings	4	3
Total contribution	£20	£6

Average contribution per unit based on above weightings = (£20 + £6)/7
= £3.714

Breakeven point = Fixed costs (£561,600)/Unit contribution (£3.714)
= 151,212 units (consisting of 86,407 units of P(4/7) and 64,805 units of E)

Breakeven point (sales value):

P = 86,407 units × £10 =	£864,070	
E = 64,805 units × £12 =	£777,660	
	£1,641,730	

(ii)

Product	P	E
Unit contribution	£5	£2
Weightings	4	4
Total contribution	£20	£8

Average contribution = (£20 + £8)/8 = £3.50
Breakeven point = £561,600/£3.50 = 160,457 units consisting of 80,228 units of each product.

Breakeven point (sales value) = (80,228 × £10) + (80,228 × £12)
= £1,765,016

(iii) The product mix in (a)(i) above is preferable because it yields the higher average contribution per unit.

(iv) Machine hours are the limiting factor and the company should concentrate on the product which maximizes the contribution per machine hour.

Product	P	E
Contribution	£5	£2
Contribution per machine hour	£12.50	£20
	(£5/0.40 hours)	(£2/0.10 hours)

The company should therefore concentrate on Product E. If all the 32,000 machine hours are allocated to Product E the profit will be as follows:

Contribution (32,000 hours at £20 per hour)	£640,000
Less fixed costs	£561,600
Profit	£78,400

(b) See Fig. 9.5 and Fig. 9.6 in Chapter 9 for an illustration of both break-even charts. The answer should stress that the contribution graph enables the contribution at any activity level to be determined and so provides more information than a conventional graph.

Answer to question 9.28

(a) *Monthly losses at minimum sales level:*

	Existing equipment		New equipment	
Unit selling price	£5.00	£3.20	£5.00	£3.20
Unit variable cost	2.60	2.60	1.00	1.00
Contribution per unit	2.40	0.60	4.00	2.20
Sales (units)	600	1,200	600	1,400
Total contribution	1,440	720	2,400	3,080
Fixed costs	1,800	1,800	4,000	4,000
Monthly loss	360	1,080	1,600	920

(b) Break-even points (units) 750 (1)   3,000 (1)   1,000 (1)   1,818 (1)

Note:
Fixed cost/contribution per unit.

(c) At the higher selling price the profits are:

Existing equipment [(1,200 × £2.40) − £1,800] = £1,080
New equipment [(1,200 × £4) − £4,000] = £800

At the lower selling price it is not possible to achieve a profit of £1,080 with the existing equipment. At the maximum level of activity of 1,200 units the answer to (a) indicates that a loss of £1,080 will be made.

If the new equipment is acquired the required profit to achieve the maximum profit at the higher selling price from the *existing* equipment is calculated as follows:

Required contribution = £1,080 planned profit + £4,000 fixed costs
                        = £5,080
Required sales volume = 2,309 units (£5,080/£2.20 contribution per unit)

The required profit to achieve the maximum profit at the higher selling price from the *new* equipment is:

Required contribution = £800 planned profit + £4,000 fixed costs = £4,800
Required sales volume = 2,182 units (£4,800/£2.20 contribution per unit)

Answer to question 9.29

Task 1

(1) Production volume (packs)	40,000	50,000	60,000	70,000
(2) Average cost	£430	£388	£360	£340
(3) Total cost (1 × 2)	£17,200,000	£19,400,000	£21,600,000	£23,800,000
(4) Cost per extra 10,000 packs		£2,200,000	£2,200,000	£2,200,000
(5) Unit variable cost ((4)/10,000)		£220	£220	£220

(a)
		£
Total cost for 40,000 packs		17,200,000
less Variable costs (40,000 × £220)		8,800,000
Fixed costs		8,400,000

(b)
Unit contribution (£420 − £220)		200
Total contribution (£200 × 65,000 packs)		13,000,000
less Fixed costs		8,400,000
Profit		4,600,000

(c) Break-even point (packs) = Fixed costs/Unit contribution = £8,400,000/£200
= 42,000

(d) Margin of safety = (65,000 − 42,000)/65,000 = 35.4%

Task 2

(a) Additional contribution = 5,000 × (£330 − £220) = £550,000
Fixed costs are assumed to remain unchanged. Therefore profits should increase by £550,000.

(b)
Additional contribution from the order =	
15,000 × (£340 − £220) =	£1,800,000
Lost contribution from current sales =	
10,000 × (£420 − £220) =	£2,000,000
Loss from the order	£200,000

(c) The order for 5,000 units at £330 should be accepted since this yields an additional contribution of £550,000. Fixed costs are assumed to remain unchanged for both orders. However, accepting an order for 15,000 units can only be met by reducing current sales by 10,000 units (planned existing sales are 65,000 units and capacity is restricted to 70,000 units). The order can only be justified if the lost sales can be recouped in future periods with no loss in customer goodwill.

(d) Non-financial factors that should be considered include:
   (i) The effect on existing customers if they become aware that the company is selling at a lower price to other customers.
   (ii) The long-term potential of the new order. If the order is likely to result in repeat sales it might be financially viable to increase capacity and obtain the increased contribution without the loss of contribution from existing sales. The financial appraisal should compare the present value of the increase in contribution with the additional costs associated with increasing capacity.

Answer to question 9.31

(a) Absorption costing unitizes fixed production overheads and includes them in the stock valuation whereas marginal costing does not include fixed overheads in the stock valuation. Instead, total fixed production overheads incurred are treated as period costs. Therefore, the total fixed overheads of £385,000 (250,000 units of A plus 100,000 units of B valued at £1.10 per unit) are charged as an expense with a marginal costing system.

Total production is 350,000 units (250,000 units of A plus 100,000 units of B) and total sales volume is 335,000 units (225,000 units of A plus 110,000 units of B). Production exceeds sales by 15,000 units resulting in an equivalent increase in stocks. With an absorption costing £16,500 (15,000 units $\times$ £1.10) out of a total fixed overheads incurred of £385,000 will be included in the stock valuation and not recorded as an expense for the current period. Therefore the cost of sales with an absorption costing system will be £16,500 lower than marginal costing cost of sales thus resulting in absorption costing showing an extra £16,500 profits for the period.

(b) Total fixed overheads for the period is calculated as follows: £
Production fixed overhead

	£
(350,000 units normal production $\times$ £1.10)	385,000
Other fixed overheads (335,000 units sales $\times$ £0.50)	167,500
	552,500

It is assumed that other fixed overheads are absorbed on the basis of sales volume rather than production volume.

The cost–volume–profit analysis should be based on the assumption that sales will be in accordance with the planned sales mix of 225,000 units of A and 110,000 units of B. This sales mix will yield the following total contribution:

	Product A	Product B	Total
(1) Selling price	5.70	6.90	
(2) Variable cost	3.45	4.80	
(3) Unit contribution	2.25	2.10	
(4) Sales volume (units)	225,000	110,000	
(5) Total contribution (3 $\times$ 4)	£506,250	£231,000	£737,250
(6) Total sales revenue (1 $\times$ 4)	£1,282,500	£759,000	£2,041,500

Average contribution per unit = £737,250/335,000 units total sales
= £2.2007
Average selling price per unit = Total sales revenue (£2,041,500)/Total sales volume (335,000) = £6.094
Break-even point (units) = Total fixed costs/Average contribution per unit
= £552,500/£2.2007
= 251,056 units
Break-even point (sales value) = 251,056 units $\times$ average selling price
(£6.094) = £1,529,935

Alternatively, the break-even point in sales value can be computed using the following formula:

$$\frac{\text{Total fixed costs (£552,500)}}{\text{Total contribution (£737,250)}} \times \text{Total sales (£2,041,500)}$$

= £1,529,913.

Measuring costs and benefits for decision-making

Answers to Chapter 10

Question summary

10.1 to 10.7
Multiple choice questions.

10.8
Make-or-buy decisions.

10.9
Determining minimum short-term acceptable selling price.

10.10 and 10.11
Comparing relevant costs with a proposed pricing quotation.

10.12
Decision on which of two mutually exclusive contracts to accept.

10.13
Decision on whether a project involving sunk and opportunity costs should be continued.

10.14 and 10.15
Determination of minimum short-run selling price adopting a relevant cost approach.

10.16 to 10.18
These questions involve deleting a segment or product abandonment decisions. Question 10.17 also involves cost–volume–profit (CVP) analysis.

10.19
A recommendation as to whether to launch a new product.

10.20 to 10.22
Determining an optimal production schedule where a limiting factor applies.

10.23
Make-or-buy decisions and limiting factors.

10.24
Allocation of shop space based on limiting factors.

10.25
A make-or-buy decision where spare capacity exists.

10.26
Limiting /key factors and a decision relating to whether it is profitable to expand output by overtime.

10.27
Price/output and key factor decisions.

10.28
Limiting factor optimum production and the use of simultaneous equations where more than one scarce factor exists.

10.29
Computation of minimum and optimum selling prices based on price/demand relationships.

Answer to question 10.9

(a) The minimum quote is equal to the relevant costs arising from the order. The relevant costs are:

	£
Raw materials:	
X: 960 kg at £3.10 per kg[a]	2,976
Y: 570 kg at £2.30 per kg[b]	1,311
Other materials	3,360
Direct labour[c]:	
2,000 hours at £4 per hour	8,000
200 hours at £5.20 per hour	1,040
Variable overhead:	
2,200 hours at £2.40 per hour	5,280
Opportunity cost:	
Overtime premium saving forgone as a result of not bringing forward production of future order (2,000 hours at £1.20 per hour)	2,400
	24,367

Notes:
[a]The original purchase cost of the materials is a sunk cost. The use of materials on this order would result in their replacement and thus represents the future impact of undertaking the order.

MEASURING COSTS AND BENEFITS FOR DECISION-MAKING

^{b}Material Y would not be replaced and if the order is not undertaken would yield revenue of £2.30 per kg. Therefore undertaking the order would result in lost sales revenue of £3,360.

^{c}The question indicates that the labour cost is avoidable if the contract is not undertaken. Thus acceptance of the contract results in additional labour costs of £9,040.

(b)   See Chapter 2 for an explanation of each of the terms.

Answer to question 10.10

(a)

	Relevant costs of the project
Material A	(1,750)
Material B	8,000
Direct labour	7,000
Net cost of machinery	4,750
Relevant cost	18,000
Contract price	30,000
Contribution	12,000

Notes:

(1) There is a saving in material costs of £1,750 if material A is not used.

(2) The actual cost of material B represents the incremental cost.

(3) The hiring of the labour on the other contract represents the additional cash flows of undertaking this contract.

(4) The net cost of purchasing the machinery represents the additional cash flows associated with the contract.

(5) Supervision and overheads will still continue even if the contract is not accepted and are therefore irrelevant.

(b)   The report should indicate that the costs given in the question do not represent incremental cash flows arising from undertaking the contract. As the company is operating at an activity level in excess of break-even point any sales revenue in excess of £18,000 incremental costs will provide an additional contribution which will result in an increase in profits. Assuming that the company has spare capacity, and that a competitor is prepared to accept the order at £30,000, then a tender price slightly below £30,000 would be appropriate.

(c)   Before accepting the contract the following non-monetary factors should be considered.

(i)   Is there sufficient spare capacity to undertake the project?

(ii)   Is the overseas customer credit worthy?

(iii)   Has the work force the necessary skills to undertake the project?

(iv)   Is the contract likely to result in repeat business with the customer?

(d)   If the company were operating below the break-even point, acceptance of the order would provide a further contribution towards fixed costs and reduce the existing loss. In the short term it is better to accept the order and reduce the total loss but if, in the long run, there are not enough orders to generate sufficient contributions to cover total fixed costs, then the company will not survive.

Answer to question 10.11

(a) The relevant costs for the production of 400 components are as follows:

	£	£
Materials:		
M1 (1200 kg at £5.50 replacement cost)	6,600	
P2 (800 kg at £2 per kg)[a]	1,600	
Part no. 678 (400 at £50 replacement cost)	20,000	28,200
Labour:		
Skilled (2,000 hours at £4 per hour)	8,000	
Semi-skilled (2,000 hours at £3 per hour)	6,000	14,000
Overheads:		
Variable (1,600 machine hours at £7 per hour)		11,200
Fixed: Incremental fixed costs		3,200
Total relevant cost		56,600
Contract price (400 components at £145 per component)		58,000
Contribution to general fixed costs		1,400

The incremental revenues exceed the incremental costs. Therefore the contract should be accepted subject to the comments in (b) below.

Note:
[a]If materials P2 are not used on the contract, they will be used as a substitute for material P4. Using P2 as a substitute for P4 results in a saving of £2 (£3.60 − £1.60) per kg. Therefore the relevant cost of P2 consists of the opportunity cost of £2 per kg.

(b) Three factors which should be considered are:
   (i) Can a price higher than £145 per component be negotiated? The contract only provides a contribution of £1,400 to general fixed costs. If the company generates insufficient contribution from its activities to cover general fixed costs then it will incur losses and will not be able to survive in the long term. It is assumed that acceptance of the contract will not lead to the rejection of other profitable work.
   (ii) Will acceptance of the contract lead to repeat orders which are likely to provide a better contribution to general fixed costs?
   (iii) Acceptance of the contract will provide additional employment for 12 months, and this might have a significant effect on the morale of the workforce.

Answer to question 10.13

(a) A direct cost is physically traceable to some cost object. The cost object is not necessarily a product; it may be, for example, a department, a cost centre or a fleet of lorries. A cost may be direct to one cost object and indirect to another.

(b)   Relevant cost
                                                                            £

   (i)   The costs incurred to date are sunk.   Nil

   (ii) The material cost of £60,000 is a sunk cost, but if the research project is undertaken then there will be a saving of disposal costs if the project continues.   (5,000)

   (iii) If the project is discontinued the labour which would have been used on the project will earn a contribution of £50,000. The labour cost of £40,000 will occur whatever alternative is selected. Therefore the company will lose £90,000 (£50,000 + £40,000) if the project continues.   90,000

   (iv) It is assumed that research salaries of £60,000 could be saved if the project is discontinued. Consequently it is a relevant cost of continuing with the project. The redundancy payment will remain unchanged if the project is discontinued.   60,000

Therefore it is not relevant. However, the redundancy payment will be made earlier if the project is discontinued. The lost interest or interest cost on this earlier payment represents a cost saving of continuing with the project. At an interest rate of 10%, there will be a saving of £2,500.   (2,500)

   (v) The general and building services is an apportioned cost which will still continue if the project is discontinued. Therefore the cost is not relevant to the decision.

	£
Total relevant costs	142,500
Relevant revenues	300,000
Contribution to fixed costs and profits	157,500

The company should continue with the project.

Answer to question 10.14

(a)   *Revised cost estimate:*

	£	
Direct materials: paper	2,500	(1)
inks	3,000	(2)
	5,500	
Direct labour (£500 + £625)	1,125	(3)
Unskilled labour	–	(4)
Variable overhead	1,400	(5)
Printing	600	(6)
Printing press depreciation	–	(7)
Fixed production costs	–	(7)
Estimating department costs	–	(8)
	8,625	

Notes:

(1)   The alternative use of the paper is to sell it for £2,500. Therefore the cash flow impact is £2,500.

(2)　The incremental cost of undertaking the work is £3,000.

(3)　It is assumed that 125 hours not undertaken at weekends is in scarce supply and the decision to undertake the work will result in a lost contribution. The relevant cost is the hourly labour rate plus the lost contribution per hour. The lost contribution is not given in the question and therefore cannot be ascertained. The hourly labour rate consisting of 125 hours at £4 per hour is included in the above answer. It is assumed that the weekend hours represent an incremental cost and do not involve a lost contribution. The incremental cost of weekend work is £625 (125 hours × £5).

(4)　At present 200 unskilled hours are recorded as idle time and the work to be undertaken entails 100 hours plus 50 hours time off in lieu. Therefore idle time will be reduced but no additional expenditure will be incurred.

(5)　It is assumed that £1,400 is an incremental cost of undertaking the work.

(6)　The lost contribution of £600 (200 hours at £3 per hour) is included in the cost estimate. It is assumed that the variable cost of the printing press hours have already been included in the cost estimate.

(7)　Fixed overheads and depreciation are fixed costs and therefore do not involve incremental cash flows.

(8)　The cost of estimating time has already been incurred and is a sunk cost.

(b)　See the section on measuring relevant costs and benefits in Chapter 10 for the answer to this question.

(c)　See the section on make-or-buy decisions in Chapter 10 and opportunity costs in Chapter 2 for the answer to this question.

Answer to question 10.19

(a)

	£	£
Direct materials:		
Material A: (30 kg/0.9) × £5.13/kg (W1)	171.00	
Others: £1.34/unit × 100	134.00	305.00
Direct labour:		
Department 1: 40 hours × £4.00/hour	160.00	
Department 2:15 hours × £4.50/hour	67.50	227.50
Production overhead:		
Department 1: Variable, 40% × £160.00	64.00	
Fixed, 90% × £160.00	144.00	
Department 2: Variable, £0.9 per DLH × 15 hours (W2)	13.50	
Fixed, £2.05 per DLH × 15 hours (W3)	30.75	252.25
Other overhead:		
Variable: £0.70 per unit × 100	70.00	
Fixed: £1.95 per unit × 100	195.00	265.00
Total cost		1,049.75

Workings:
(W1)　2,400,000 × 30/0.9 per 100 kg = 800,000 purchases p.a.
= 66,667 per month

(*W2*) Department 2 overhead:

Variable	£1,980,000
Fixed	£3,444,000 (balance)
	£5,424,000

Variable overhead rate = £1,980,000/2,200,000 hours
= £0.90 per direct labour hour

(*W3*) Expected usage of direct labour hours:
Expected capacity
(excluding new product) = 1.32 million hours (0.6 × 2.2 m)
Capacity required for
new product = 0.36 million hours (2.4 m × 15/100)
Total hours 1.68

Fixed overhead rate = £3,444,000/1,680,000 direct labour hours
= £2.05 per direct labour hour

(b) The total cost per unit of £10.50 (£1,049.75/100) is below the expected selling price of £9.95 and it appears that the product is not profitable. However, the new product provides a contribution of £3.15 per unit towards fixed costs. The calculation is as follows:

	£
Variable costs:	
Direct materials	3.05
Direct labour	2.275
Variable production overhead	0.775
Other variable overhead	0.70
	6.80
Selling price	9.95
Contribution	3.15

A total annual contribution of £7.56 m (£3.15 × 2.4 m annual sales) towards fixed costs will be obtained if the new product is introduced. If fixed costs will not be affected by the decision to introduce the new product then the new product should be launched because it will provide an annual contribution of £7.5 m which would not otherwise be obtained. The company is currently working at 60% capacity and, with the introduction of the new product, utilization of available capacity will be increased to 76% (1.68 m hours/2.2 m maximum capacity). Therefore sufficient capacity is available to meet the demand for the new product and no opportunity cost is involved resulting from a need to reduce existing output.

With the introduction of the new product, spare capacity would remain, and the company should seek to utilize this capacity with other profitable work. If no other profitable work is likely to be obtained in the long term, then the company should consider reducing capacity to either 60% or 76% of existing capacity. If the annual fixed costs that can be saved from reducing capacity from 76% to 60% exceed the £7.56 m contribution generated by the new product then it is more profitable to reduce capacity to 60% and not introduce the new product.

(c) At a selling price of £9.45 per unit, contribution per unit will be reduced by £0.50, and the annual contribution will be £7.685 (£2.65 × 2.9 m sales). At a selling price of £9.95 the expected contribution is £7.56 m. It is therefore more profitable to reduce selling price if management are confident that the price reduction will increase sales volume by 500,000 units (approximately 20%) and will not affect the selling prices of other products. There is sufficient capacity to meet the additional sales volume and it is assumed that the increase in demand will not result in a change in fixed costs.

Answer to question 10.22

(a)

Products	701	702	821	822	937
Selling price	£26.00	£28.00	£34.00	£38.00	£40.00
Variable costs:					
Direct materials	5.60	4.00	11.20	10.40	12.00
Direct labour	5.00	4.00	7.50	5.50	7.00
Variable overheads	2.00	1.60	3.00	2.20	2.80
Selling overhead	3.90	4.20	5.10	5.70	6.00
Contribution	9.50	14.20	7.20	14.20	12.20
Contribution per kg of materials	13.57	28.4	5.14	10.92	8.13
Ranking	2	1	5	3	4

Allocation of materials:

Product	Units	Material used (kg)	Unused materials (kg)
702	7,200	3,600	13,400
701	8,000	5,600	7,800
822	6,000	7,800	–

(b) *Contribution and profit:*

Product	702	701	822	Total
	£	£	£	£
Contribution	102,240	76,000	85,200	263,440
Fixed production overhead (1)	17,280	24,000	19,800	61,080
Fixed selling overhead (2)				75,000
Net profit				127,360

Notes:
(1) Fixed overhead absorbed is equal to fixed overhead incurred and is absorbed at the rate of 60% of direct labour cost (702 = 7,200 × £2.40; 701 = 8,000 × £3; 822 = 6,000 × £3.30).
(2) 1/4 × Annual fixed overheads (£300,000).

(c) The analysis used in (a) is based on the techniques described in Chapter 10 in the section relating to decision-making and the influence of key factors. This type of analysis is appropriate whenever sales demand is in excess of the company's productive capacity so that the factor responsible for limiting output can be identified and the greatest possible contribution to profit is obtained each time the scarce or limiting factor is used. Other examples of business problems where this type of analysis can be useful include:
  (i) optimizing the use of labour where output is restricted by shortage of labour;

(ii) optimizing the hours of machine time available where output is restricted by machine hours;

(iii) optimizing the use of space where sales are restricted because of lack of space;

(iv) make-or-buy decisions involving limiting factors (see Questions 10.20–10.22).

Answer to question 10.24

(a)

	(i) Contribution 1 module £	(ii) Contribution per module 2 modules £	(iii) Total contribution from 2 modules £	(iv) Incremental contribution from second module, (iii)–(i) £
Range A (20% of sales)	1,350 (3)	1,250	2,500	1,150 (5)
B (40% of sales)	1,400 (2)	1,260	2,520	1,120 (6)
C (25% of sales)	1,200 (4)	1,150	2,300	1,100 (7)
D (25% of sales)	1,600 (1)	1,300	2,600	1,000
E (30% of sales)	1,000	1,100	2,200	1,200

The numbers (1)–(4) refer to the ranking of modules by contributions. Note that the high contribution on the second module for range E is dependent upon two modules being allocated. The first module cannot be justified on its own, and the two together provide a lower allocation than two modules allocated for ranges A, B and C. Thus the allocation of the modules is as follows:

Range D – 1st module
B – 1st module
A – 1st module
C – 1st module
A – 2nd module
B – 2nd module
C – 2nd module

(b) Profits per week:

	Contribution £	Operating costs £	Profit £
Range A	2,500	1,600	900
B	2,520	1,600	920
C	2,300	1,600	700
D	1,600	800	800
	8,920	5,600	3,320

(c) See the section on decision-making and the influence of limiting factors in Chapter 10 for the answer to this question.

Answer to question 10.25

(a)

	C £	D £
Selling price	127	161
Variable costs	66	87
Contribution	61	74

The drilling and grinding hours required to meet the production requirements for the period are calculated as follows:

	A	B	C	D	Total
Hours per unit: Drilling	2	1	3	4	
Grinding	2	4	1	3	
Units of output	50	100	250	500	
Drilling hours required	100	100	750	2,000	2,950
Grinding hours required	100	400	250	1,500	2,250

Drilling hours are the limiting factor (1,650 hours are available). The contributions per drilling hour are £20.33 for product C (£61/3 hours) and £18.50 (£74/4 hours) for product D. Therefore the maximum demand of product C should be met, resulting in 950 drilling hours being utilized (750 for product C and 200 hours for components A and B). The remaining capacity of 700 hours can be used to produce 175 units of product D. It is assumed that the internal demand for components A and B must have priority over meeting the demand for product D. The estimated profit per week is:

	£
Contribution from product C (250 units at £61)	15,250
Contribution from product D (175 units at £74)	12,950
Total contribution	28,200
Allocated fixed overheads (250 × £23) + (175 × £39)	12,575
	15,625

(b) (i) Components A and B are not used to produce either of the finished products but if they are purchased drilling time can be freed up to expand production of product D. The variable costs of components A and B are £32 and £78 respectively and the outside purchasing costs are £50 and £96. Thus variable costs will increase by £18 per unit for both components but the contribution per drilling hour from producing product D is £18.50. Purchase of component A releases 2 drilling hours (yielding £37 additional product D contribution) and purchase of component B releases 1 drilling hour (yielding £18.50 additional contribution). Thus components A and B should be purchased from outside and this will free up 200 drilling hours (50 components × 2 hours for component A plus 100 × 1 hour for component B). This will enable output of product D to be expanded by 50 units (200 hours/4 hours per unit). The increase in contribution is calculated as follows:

	£	£
Additional contribution from Product D (50 × £74)		3,700
Less additional purchasing costs:		
Component A (50 × £18)	900	
Component B (100 × £18)	1,800	2,700
Additional contribution		1,000

(ii) For the answer to this question see the sections on single-resource constraints and two-resource constraints in Chapter 25 of *Management and Cost Accounting* (Fourth edition) written by the author (International Thomson Business Press, 1996).

Answer to question 10.26

(a) Machine hours are the limiting factor and profits will be maximized by allocating machine hours on the basis of a product's contribution per machine hour. In order to do this it is necessary to compute the output per machine hour for each product.

Calculation of output per machine hour:

$$\text{Manufacturing overhead rate} = £427,500/2,250 \text{ hrs}$$
$$= £190 \text{ per machine hour}$$

$$\text{Output per machine hour} = \frac{\text{machine hour rate}}{\text{overhead allocated per unit of output}}$$

Product W = 222.2 (£190/£0.855) units per hour
X = 200 (£190/£0.950) units per hour
Y = 400 (£190/£0.475) units per hour
Z = 250 (£190/£0.76) units per hour

Calculation of contribution per machine hour:

	Product			
	W	X	Y	Z
	£	£	£	£
Selling price per unit	3.650	3.900	2.250	2.950
Variable costs per unit	1.865	2.110	1.272	1.589
Contribution per unit	1.785	1.790	0.978	1.361
Output per machine hour (units)	222.2	200	400	250
Contribution per machine hour (£)	396.6	358	391.2	340.25
Ranking	1	3	2	4

Required machine hours to meet the maximum demand:

Product W = 855 hours (190,000/222.2)
X = 625 hours (125,000/200)
Y = 360 hours (144,000/400)
Z = 568 hours £142,000/250)
2,408 hours

Practical capacity is only 2,250 machine hours and therefore there is a shortfall of 158 hours. Output of product Z should be reduced by 39,500 units (158 hours × 250 units per hour). The optimum output schedule is to produce 102,500 (142,000 − 39,500) units of product Z and maximum demand as per the sales forecast for products W, X and Z.

(b) *Calculation of profits with overtime:*

	Product				Total
	W	X	Y	Z	£
Sales volume (units)	190,000	125,000	144,000	142,000	
Contribution per unit (£)	1.785	1.790	0.978	1.361	
Total contribution (excluding overtime premium)	339,150	223,750	140,832	193,262	896,994
Less overtime premium[a]					(10,053)
					886,941
Less fixed costs.					
Manufacturing					(427,500)
Selling and administration					(190,000)
Additional					(24,570)
Net profit					244,871

Note:

[a]The production shortfall of 158 machine hours could be made up by working overtime on any of the four products.

The direct labour cost per machine hour for each product is:

$$\text{Product W} = £134.20 \ (222.2 \times £0.604)$$
$$\text{X} = £130.20 \ (200 \times £0.651)$$
$$\text{Y} = £162 \ (400 \times £0.405)$$
$$\text{Z} = £127.25 \ (250 \times £0.509)$$

Therefore it is cheaper to work overtime on product Z.
The overtime premium will be $39,500 \times (£0.509 \times 0.5)$

(c)

	£
Additional contribution from working overtime on product Z (39,500 units × £1.361)	53,759
Less:	
Overtime premium	(10,053)
Additional fixed costs	(24,570)
Additional profit	19,136

Prior to making the decision management should ensure that staff are prepared to work overtime and that this will not result in lower productivity due to working longer hours.

Answer to question 10.29

(a) The minimum selling price should cover incremental costs of meeting the order. It is assumed that labour is an incremental cost and that none of the fixed overheads would be avoidable if a batch of 200 units was not produced.
The total cost per unit is £61.92 (£31.65 + £21.82 + £3.05 + £5.40). The

fixed cost per unit is £7.84 (£3 + £2.50 + £1.50 + £0.84). Therefore the incremental cost per unit (excluding set-up cost) is £54.08 (£61.92 − £7.84) The incremental cost of a batch of 200 units is £10,816 (£54.08 × 200) plus set-up cost (£20) = £10,836.

The above selling price does not generate a contribution towards fixed costs. In order to make a profit a price should be set that ensures that a contribution is made towards fixed costs.

Adopting a selling price based on a margin above variable cost does not take into account customer demand or competitors' selling prices for similar products. Any attempt to price below competitors should consider their reactions as they may meet the selling price reduction and thus market prices will fall. The overall effect will be the same market share at a lower selling price.

The company also must consider the impact on customer goodwill once its other customers become aware of the special price that is being charged to key customers.

(b) Assuming that all of the fixed costs are unavoidable, and the released capacity has no alternative use if the company sub-contracts the product, the incremental costs of making the product are the variable costs of £6.20 per box. This is lower than the sub-contract price and the company should therefore make the first 7,000 units itself. The estimated total contribution for each selling price is as follows:

Selling price £	Demand	Unit variable cost £	Unit contribution £	Total contribution £
13	5,000	6.20	6.80	34,000
12	6,000	6.20	5.80	34,800
11	7,000	6.20	4.80	33,600
	200	7.75	3.25	650
				34,250
10	7,000	6.20	3.80	26,600
	4,200	7.75	2.25	9,450
				36,050
9	7,000	6.20	2.80	19,600
	6,400	7.00	2.00	12,800
				32,400

Profits are maximized at a selling price of £10 per unit.

(c) Management should consider ways of utilizing the limiting factor more efficiently. Examples include:

(i) improving product design in order to reduce the usage of labour, materials or machinery;

(ii) improving production methods, plant layout or machine usage in order to avoid bottlenecks so that output can be increased from the existing facilities;

(iii) introducing overtime where labour is the limiting factor;

(iv) sub-contracting the manufacturing of components or products in order to 'free up' capacity.

Activity-based costing

Answers to Chapter 11

Question summary

ABC did not emerge until the late 1980s, and therefore very few examination questions have been set on this topic. This chapter contains five questions:

11.1 and 11.2
Essay questions.

11.3 to 11.7
A comparison of product costs derived from traditional and activity-based costing is required. Question 11.6 also requires the preparation of conventional costing and ABC costing profit statements.

Answer to question 11.1

The answer to this question should describe cost allocation, cost apportionment and absorption within a traditional product costing system. Both traditional and ABC systems use the two-stage allocation procedure. In the first stage costs are assigned to cost centres and in the second stage costs are charged to products passing through the cost centres using appropriate overhead absorption rates.

The terms 'cost allocation' and 'cost apportionment' are often used interchangeably to describe methods that are used in the first stage to arbitrarily share out costs to cost centres on some logical basis (e.g. rent may be apportioned on the basis of floor area of each department and works management on the basis of number of employees in each department). However, some textbooks distinguish between the two terms. Allocations are used to describe those overheads that can be specifically attributed to a cost centre (e.g. depreciation of machinery or the wages of a supervisor located in a specific cost centre). The term 'apportionment' is used where a cost cannot be specifically attributed to a cost centre and the costs have to be apportioned on some logical basis (e.g. rent apportioned to cost centres on the basis of floor area).

The term 'absorption' is normally used to refer to the second stage of the two-stage overheads process by which cost centre overheads are charged to products (i.e. absorbed by products) passing through the cost centre. Direct labour hours or machine hours are the most widely used absorption methods to assign the cost centre overheads to products.

The answer should then go on to describe activity-based costing systems and also the limitations of traditional product costing systems (see Chapter 11 for a description of ABC).

Answer to question 11.3

For the answer to this question see the sections on limitations of traditional cost systems, an illustration of ABC and traditional costing systems and impact of volume diversity in Chapter 11.

Answer to question 11.5

(a) *Production cost per unit (conventional method):*

	Product X	Product Y	Product Z
	£	£	£
Direct labour at £6 per hour	3	9	6
Direct materials	20	12	25
Production overhead at £28 per machine hour	42 ($1\frac{1}{2}$ hours)	28 (1 hour)	84 (3 hours)
	65	49	115

(b) The total production overhead is derived from the overheads allocated to the product in part (a):

	£	
Product X	31,500	(750 × £42)
Product Y	35,000	(1,250 × £28)
Product Z	588,000	(7000 × £84)
	654,500	

Overhead costs traced to cost pools:

	£	
Set-up cost	229,075	(35%)
Machining	130,900	(20%)
Materials handling	98,175	(15%)
Inspection	196,350	(30%)
	654,500	

Cost driver rates:

	£	
Cost per set-up	341.903	(£229,075/670)
Cost per machine hour	5.60	(£130,900/23,375[a])
Cost per material movement	818.125	(£98,175/120)
Cost per inspection	196.35	(£196,350/1,000)

Note:

Machine hours = $(750 \times 1\frac{1}{2}) + (1{,}250 \times 1) + (7{,}000 \times 3) = 23{,}375$

Overhead cost assigned to each product:

	Product X £	Product Y £	Product Z £
Set-up costs at £341.903	25,643 (75)	39,319 (115)	164,113 (480)
Machining at £5.60 per machine hour	6,300 (1,125)	7,000 (1,250)	117,600 (21,000)
Materials handling at £818.125 per movement	9,817 (12)	17,181 (21)	71,177 (87)
Inspection at £196.35 per inspection	29,453 (150)	35,343 (180)	131,554 (670)
	71,213	98,843	484,444
Number of units	750	1,250	7,000
Overhead cost per unit	£95	£79	£69

Production cost per unit (ABC principles):

	Product X £	Product Y £	Product Z £
Direct labour	3	9	6
Materials	20	12	25
Production overhead	95	79	69
	118	100	100
Change (compared with traditional method)	+82%	+104%	−13%

(c) The traditional method allocates overheads in proportion to machine hours to products (4.8% to X, 5.3% to Y and 89.9% to Z). However, when overheads are assigned on the basis of number of set-ups, movements of materials and inspections the proportion of overheads assigned to product Z are 72% (480/670) for set-up costs, 72% (87/120) for materials handling costs and 67% (670/1,000) for inspection costs. In contrast, the traditional method allocates approximately 90% of all costs to product Z. Therefore the unit cost for product Z is higher with the traditional method. The opposite situation applies with products X and Y and, as a result, unit costs are lower with the traditional method.

Answer to question 11.7

(i) *Tradition volume-based system:*
The first stage of the two-stage overhead allocation procedure requires that the service department overheads are reallocated to the production depart-ments (Machinery and Fittings). Typical allocation bases are:

Materials handling	– Direct material cost	
Material procurement	– Direct material cost	
Set-up	– Direct labour hours	
Maintenance	– Machine cost or maintenance hours	
Quality control	– Direct labour hours	

It is assumed that the £10,500 service department costs will be apportioned as follows:

	£000
Machinery	6,500
Fittings	4,000

(Note that students will require details of the above allocation since the details are not given in the question.)

The computation of the departmental overhead rates is as follows:

	Machinery department £	Fitting department £
Original overhead allocation	2,500,000	2,000,000
Service department reallocations	6,500,000	4,000,000
Total production overhead cost (£)	9,000,000	6,000,000
Total direct labour hours	1,100,000	350,000
Overhead rate	£8.182 per DLH	£17.143 per DLH

Product costs:

	Product A £	Product B £
Machinery department:		
500,000 DLH × £8.182	4,091,000	
600,000 DLH × £8.182		4,909,200
Fitting department:		
150,000 DLH × £17.143	2,571,500	
200,000 DLH × £17.143		3,428,600
Total production overhead cost (£)	6,662,500	8,337,800
Production volume (£)	300,000	300,000
Unit product overhead cost (£)	22.21	27.79

(ii) *Activity-based costing system:*

Computation of cost driver rates:

Overhead	Annual cost £000	Annual cost driver volume	Cost driver rate
Material handling	1,500	2,540 material movements	£590.55 per material movement
Material procurement	2,000	6,500 orders	£307.69 per order
Set-up	1,500	624 set-ups	£2,403.85 per set-up
Maintenance	2,500	30,000 maintenance hours	£83.33 per maintenance per hour
Quality control	3,000	4,120 inspections	£728.16 per inspection
Machinery	2,500	1,100,000 direct labour hours	£2.27 per DLH
Fitting	2,000	350,000 direct labour hours	£5.71 per DLH

Overheads assigned to part numbers:

	Material handling	Material procurement	Set-up	Maintenance	Quality Control	Machinery	Fitting	Total £000
Part 1:								
Cost driver consumption	180	200	12	7,000	360	150,000	50,000	
Cost driver rate (£)	590.55	307.69	2,403.85	83.33	728.16	2.27	5.71	
Total cost (£000)	106.30	61.54	28.85	583.31	262.14	340.50	285.50	1,668
Part 2:								
Cost driver consumption	160	300	12	5,000	360	350,000	100,000	
Cost driver rate (£)	590.55	307.69	2,403.85	83.33	728.16	2.27	5.71	
Total cost (£000)	94.49	92.31	28.85	416.65	262.14	794.50	571.00	2,260
Part 3:								
Cost driver consumption	1,000	2,000	300	10,000	2,400	200,000	60,000	
Cost driver rate (£)	590.55	307.69	2,403.85	83.33	728.16	2.27	5.71	
Total cost (£000)	590.55	615.38	721.16	833.30	1,747.58	454.00	342.60	5,305
Part 4:								
Cost driver consumption	1,200	4,000	300	8,000	1,000	400,000	140,000	
Cost driver rate (£)	590.55	307.69	2,403.85	83.33	728.16	2.27	5.71	
Total cost (£000)	708.66	1,203.76	721.16	666.64	728.16	908.00	799.40	5,763

Product costs:

	Product A £	Product B £
Part 1	1,668,000	
Part 2	2,260,000	
Part 3		5,305,000
Part 4		5,763,000
Production overhead cost (£)	3,928,000	11,068,000
Production volume	300,000 units	300,000 units
Unit cost (£)	13.09	36.89

This answer is adapted from Innes, J. and Mitchell, F. (1990) *Activity Based Costing: A review with case studies*, Chartered Institute of Management Accountants, London.

Capital investment decisions

Answers to Chapter 12

Question summary

12.1
Payback and NPV calculations.

12.2
Calculation of internal rate of return (IRR) with equal annual cash flows.

12.3
Calculation of accounting rate of return and NPV.

12.4
Part (a) requires the calculation of the NPV and the payback period. Part (b) is concerned with a machine replacement decision. The cost savings of replacing the machine are regarded as cash inflows and the revenues are considered to be irrelevant since they are the same for the existing and the replacement machine.

12.5
Calculation of NPV and payback.

12.6
Present value of purchasing or renting machinery.

12.7 to 12.11
These questions require the calculation of payback, accounting rate of return and net present value, and in most cases, require a recommendation as to which project should be accepted.

12.12
Computation of NPV and tax payable.

Answer to question 12.3

(a) (i)

$$\text{Average accounting profit} = \frac{12{,}500 \times 4 \text{ years} \times £20}{5 \text{ years}} = £200{,}000$$

$$\text{Average capital employed} = \frac{£1{,}500{,}000 + £100{,}000}{2} = £800{,}000$$

Accounting rate of return = 25% (£200,000/£800,000)

(ii) Depreciation and the allocation of general fixed overheads are not relevant to the decision. The annual cash flows are £625,000 (12,500 × £50). The NPV calculation is as follows:

Years	Cash flow £	Discount factor	PV £
1	0		0
2–4	625,000	1.755	1,096,875
5	725,000	0.402	291,450
			1,388,325
		Less initial outlay	1,500,000
		NPV	£(111,675)

(b) The project should be rejected because it has a negative NPV. See the sections on the concept of net present value and accounting rate of return in Chapter 12 for a discussion of the relative merits of each method.

Answer to question 12.5

Task 1:

(a)

Year	Cash flow £	Discount factor	Present value £
1	18,000	0.926	16,668
2	29,000	0.857	24,853
3	31,000	0.794	24,614
			66,135
	Less investment outlay		55,000
			11,135

(b) Payback occurs during the third year. Assuming even cash flows throughout the year the payback period is:

$$2 \text{ years} + \frac{(£55{,}000 - £47{,}000)}{£31{,}000} = \text{Approximately 2.3 years}$$

Task 2:

(a) The proposal should be accepted because it has a positive net present value.

(b) See the sections on the concept of net present value and payback method in Chapter 12 for the answer to this question.

(c) The answer should draw attention to the following points:

(i) Incremental profits arising from a project are taxable. The tax is normally payable approximately 12 months after the receipt of the associated cash inflows and taxation should therefore be recorded as a cash outflow in the appraisal with a time lag of 12 months.

(ii) Depreciation is not an allowable expense for taxation purposes. Instead, the Inland Revenue specifies depreciation schedules (known as capital allowances or writing down allowances) that must be used to compute taxable profits. Incremental taxation on project cash flows are therefore normally determined by multiplying the incremental profits arising from a project (cash inflows less cash outflows (excluding depreciation) less capital allowances) by the company's taxation rate.

Answer to question 12.6

(a) Machine A

End of year	Volume	Variable costs (£)	Fixed costs (£)	Cash flow (£)	Discount factors	Present value (£)
1	145,200(1)	726,000	20,000	746,000	0.870	649,020
2	159,720	798,600	20,000	818,600	0.756	618,862
3	175,692	878,460	20,000	898,460	0.658	591,187
						1,859,069
Capital cost						60,000
						1,919,069

Machine B

End of year	Volume	Variable costs (£)	Fixed costs (£)	Cash flow (£)	Discount factors	Present value (£)
1	145,200	755,040	38,000	793,040	0.870	689,945
2	159,720	830,544	38,000	868,544	0.756	656,619
3	170,000	884,000	38,000	922,000	0.658	606,676
3	5,692	56,920		56,920	0.658	37,453
						1,990,693

Note:
(1) Annual growth rate = 12,000/120,000 = 10%.

(b) Machine A should be purchased because it has the lowest present value of cash outflows. Sales revenues are irrelevant because the cash inflows are identical for both machines. A benefit that has not been quantified in the above analysis is Machine A's surplus capacity which provides a safeguard should demand be under-estimated.

(c) Because the machine must be replaced the £10,000 sale proceeds will occur whichever alternative the company chooses. Therefore the sale proceeds are not relevant for decision-making.

(d) See the sections on compounding and discounting and the concept of net present value in Chapter 12 for the answer to this question.

Answer to question 12.8

(a) *Cumulative cash flows:*

	A £	B £	C £
Year 1	80,000	100,000	55,000
2	150,000	170,000	120,000
3	215,000	220,000	215,000
4		270,000	

Payback periods:

$$\text{Project A} = 2 \text{ years} + \frac{200 - 150}{165} = 2.77 \text{ years}$$

$$\text{Project B} = 3 \text{ years} + \frac{230 - 220}{50} = 3.2 \text{ years}$$

$$\text{Project C} = 2 \text{ years} + \frac{180 - 120}{95} = 2.63 \text{ years}$$

(b)
$$\text{Accounting rate of return} = \frac{\text{Average profits}}{\text{Average investment}}$$

Average profits = Total net annual cash inflows/asset life

$$A = (330 + 10 - 200)/5 = £28,000$$
$$B = (320 + 15 - 230)/5 = £21,000$$
$$C = (315 + 8 - 180)/4 = £35,750$$

Assuming that depreciation is charged on the straight line basis:

Average investment = (Initial investment + Scrap value)/2

$$A = 210/2 = £105,000$$
$$B = 245/2 = £122,500$$
$$C = 188/2 = £94,000$$

Accounting rate of return:

$$A = £28,000/£105,000 = 26.67\%$$
$$B = £21,000/122,500 = 17.14\%$$
$$C = £35,750/£94,000 = 38.03\%$$

(c)

Project A	Outflow	Inflows	Discount factor	Present value
Year 0	−200,000	–	1.00	−200,000
1		+80,000	0.8475	+67,800
2		−70,000	0.7182	+50,274
3		+65,000	0.6086	+39,559
4		+60,000	0.5158	+30,948
5		+65,000	0.4371	+28,411
				+16,992

Project B

Year				
0	−230,000		1.00	−230,000
1		+100,000	0.8475	+84,750
2		+70,000	0.7182	+50,274
3		+50,000	0.6086	+30,430
4		+50,000	0.5158	+25,790
5		+65,000	0.4371	+28,411
				−10,345

Project C

Year				
0	−180,000		1.00	−180,000
1		+55,000	0.8475	+46,613
2		+65,000	0.7182	+46,683
3		+95,000	0.6086	+57,817
4		+108,000	0.5158	+55,706
				+26,819

(d) The NPV method of evaluation is superior to the other methods and the project with the largest NPV ought to be selected: Project C. It should be noted that Project C is also preferred to A and B when the payback and accounting rate of return methods are used.

(e) Other factors which should be considered are qualitative factors such as the impact on existing sales, the effect on employees and the effect on the environment from each of the three projects. In addition, the risk and reliability of the cash flows for each project should be considered.

Answer to question 12.10

(a) Payback and net present value are techniques which focus on cash flows rather than profits. The investment outlay is brought into the analysis as a cash flow. Depreciation should not therefore be included in the analysis as this would involve double counting. The accounting rate of return measures average profit as a percentage return on the average investment over a project's life. Because the focus is on profits, and not cash flows, depreciation should be included in the accounting rate of return computation.

(b) (i) *Payback:*

Project 1 = 2 years (£150,000 − £110,000)/£45,000 = 2.89 years
Project 2 = 3 years (£150,000 − £137,000)/£49,000 = 3.27 years

(ii) *Accounting rate of return:*

	Project 1	Project 2
Average profits	£32,500 (£130,000/4)	£28,000 (£140,000/5)
Average investment (1)	£110,000	£90,000
Accounting rate of return	30%	31%

Note:
(1) Average investment = ($\frac{1}{2}$ Investment outlay) + ($\frac{1}{2}$ Disposal value)

(iii) *Net present value:*

Year	Discount Factor	Project 1 Cash flow £	Project 1 Present value £	Project 2 Cash flow £	Project 2 Present value £
1	0.869	60,000	52,140	54,000	46,926
2	0.756	50,000	37,800	44,000	33,264
3	0.659	45,000	29,655	39,000	25,701
4	0.571	125,000	71,375	49,000	27,979
5	0.497			104,000	51,688
			190,970		185,558
Less investment outlay			150,000		150,000
NPV			40,970		35,558

The decision should be based on the NPV method and Project 1 should be chosen.

(c) The NPV method computes the present value of cash flows. Depreciation is not a cash flow whereas the disposal value at the end of the project's life is a cash flow. The payback method also focuses on cash flows and the disposal value is required to determine the average investment to compute the accounting rate of return.

Answer to question 12.11

(a)

	Cash flow				
Year	1	2	3	4	5
Saving in Fleet Costs	250,000	275,000	302,500	332,750	366,025
Less: Driver's Costs	33,000	35,000	36,000	38,000	40,000
Repairs and Maintenance	8,000	13,000	15,000	16,000	18,000
Other Costs	10,000	15,000	20,000	16,000	22,000
	51,000	63,000	71,000	70,000	80,000
Net savings	199,000	212,000	231,500	262,750	286,025

Depreciation of £120,000 per annum (£750,000 less £150,000 scrap value depreciated over 5 years) has been deducted from other costs since it is not a cash expense.

(b) (i) Payback = 3 years + (£750,000 − £642,500)/262,750
                   = 3.41 years

   (ii) Accounting Rate of Return = Average profit (£118,255)/Average investment (£450,000) = 26.3%

$$\text{Average profit} = \frac{\text{Savings over 5 years} - \text{Depreciation}}{5 \text{ years}}$$

$$= (£1,191,275 - £600,000)/5 \text{ years}$$

$$= £118,255$$

Average investment = 1/2 initial outlay + 1/2 scrap value

$$= 1/2 (£750,000) + 1/2 (150,000)$$

$$= £450,000$$

(iii) *Net present value:*

		Cost	Discount factor	£
Year 0				(750,000)
1 Saving		199,000	0.893	177,707
2 Saving		212,000	0.797	168,964
3 Saving		231,500	0.712	164,828
4 Saving		262,750	0.636	167,109
5 Saving		286,025	0.567	162,176
5 Sale of				
proceeds		150,000	0.567	85,050
Net present value				175,834

(c) The answer should draw attention to the fact that the transport fleet investment has a higher NPV but a longer payback and lower accounting rate of
return than the alternative. The decision should be based on the NPV rule and
it is recommended that the company invests in the new transport fleet. The
answer should also explain the superiority of the NPV technique over the
accounting rate of return and payback methods (see the sections on the concept of NPV, payback method and accounting rate of return in Chapter 12).

The budgeting process

Answers to Chapter 13

Question summary

13.1 to 13.5
Multiple choice questions.

13.6 and 13.7
Discussion questions relating to budgeting.

13.8 to 13.14
Preparation of cash budgets. Question 13.14 is the most difficult. Question 13.8 also requires the preparation of the budgeted profit and loss account and balance sheet and 13.11 involves the calculation of stock, debtor and creditor balances.

13.15 to 13.20
Preparation of functional budgets. Question 13.19 also requires the calculation of sales to achieve a target profit and 13.20 involves the computation of a standard product cost.

13.21
Preparation of materials purchase and usage budget and journal entries for a standard costing system.

13.22
Preparation of functional budgets, cash budget and budgeted profit and loss account and balance sheet.

13.23
Calculation of the number of budgeted direct labour employees required to meet budgeted production plus the calculation of product direct labour costs.

13.24
Preparation of functional budgets and comments on sales forecasting methods.

13.25
Construction of a model in the form of equations for the preparation of a cash budget.

Answer to question 13.6

(a) See section on why do we produce budgets in Chapter 13 for the answer to this problem.

(b) See sections on administration of the annual budget and stages in the budget process in Chapter 13 for the answer to this problem.

Answer to question 13.7

(a) See the section on stages in the budget process in Chapter 13 for the answer to this question.

(b) See the section on computerized budgeting in Chapter 13 for the answer to this part of the question.

Answer to question 13.10

(a) Cash budgets

	January £000	February £000	March £000
Balance b/f	1,450	48	412
Sales receipts	1,195	1,190	1,090
	2,645	1,238	1,502
Less			
Wages and salaries	60	60	60
Materials	240	210	240
Production overheads	424	357	375
Selling overheads	110	115	115
Corporation Tax	750		
Dividend			500
VAT	13	84	58
Capital expenditure	1,000		700
Cash outflow	2.597	826	2.048
Balance c/fwd	48	412	(546)

Workings:

	January £000	February £000	March £000
		Month of Receipt	
November	55 (5% × 1,100)	–	–
December	300 (30% × 1,000)	50 (5% × 1,000)	–
January	840 (60% × 1,400)	420 (30% × 400)	70 (5% × 1,400)
February	–	720 (60% × 1,200)	360 (30% × 1,200)
March	–	–	660 (60% × 1,100)
	1,195	1.190	1,090

Production overheads

	January £000	February £000	March £000
Prior month variable	224 (35% × 640)	196 (35% × 560)	175 (35% × 500)
Current month fixed (1)	200	161	200
	424	357	375

Note:

(1) (65% × production overheads) − £164.

VAT payable:

	January £000	February £000	March £000
Output Tax			
December sales	149	–	–
January sales	–	209	–
February sales	–	–	179
InputTax	(136)	(125)	(121)
Net payable	13	84	58

(b) (i) A permanent improvement in cash flow can be achieved by:
   (1) issuing new shares or raising long-term capital;
   (2) improving credit control procedures so that bad debts are reduced and also encouraging debtors to pay more promptly;
   (3) ensuring that any cash surpluses are invested so that they earn an appropriate rate of interest rather than lying idle;
   (4) reducing stock levels.

(ii) A temporary improvement in cash flow could be achieved by:
   (1) negotiating a delay in payments of creditors;
   (2) trying to delay the delivery of the machinery or arranging for the payments to be deferred over a longer period.

Answer to question 13.13

(a) *Cash budget (£000):*

Week	1	2	3	4	5	6
Cash receipts from sales (1)	80	80	75	70	70	80
Cash payments:						
Materials (2)	27	46	12	–	–	–
Direct labour and variable overhead (3)	41	41	16	16	16	16
Fixed overhead(4)	16	16	12	12	12	12
	84	103	40	28	28	28

Week	1	2	3	4	5	6
Weekly surplus/(deficit)	(4)	(23)	35	42	42	52
Opening cash balance	(39)	(43)	(66)	(31)	11	53
Closing cash balance	(43)	(66)	(31)	11	53	105

Notes:

(1)

Week	1	2	3	4	5	6
Opening debtors	80	40				
Week 1 sales		40	40			
2			35	35		
3				35	35	
4					35	35
5						45
	80	80	75	70	70	80

The above sales can be achieved because opening stocks of finished goods (2,800 units) + production in weeks 1 and 2 (2,400 units) are greater than sales in weeks 1 to 5 (3,800 units) by 1,400 units.

(2) *Purchase of materials:*

	Week 1 £	Week 2 £	
Closing stock	40,000	10,000	
+ Production	42,000	42,000	
(1,200 × £35)			
− Opening stock	(36,000)	(40,000)	
= Purchases	£46,000	£12,000	(paid for 1 week later)

(3)

		£	
Weeks 1 and 2 = 1,200 × 30	=	36,000	
	+	5,000	(overtime premium)
		41,000	
Weeks 3 to 6 = 800 × 20	=	16,000	

(4)

		£	
Weeks 1 and 2 = 800 × 25	=	20,000	
	−	4,000	(depreciation)
		16,000	
Weeks 3 to 6 = £16,000 − £4,000	=	12,000	

(b) The matters which should be drawn to the attention of the management are:
   (i) The overdraft limit will be exceeded in week 2 and arrangements should be made to increase this limit.
   (ii) Excess funds will be available from weeks 4–6 and plans should be made to invest these funds on a short-term basis.
   (iii) Funds will be required as soon as production recommences in order to re-establish stocks of raw materials and finished goods.

Answer to question 13.14

Quarterly cash budget for year ending 30 November 1983:

	Qtr 1 £000	Qtr 2 £000	Qtr 3 £000	Qtr4 £000
Receipts from debtors (1)	62.00	70.00	82.00	88.00

Payments:

	Qtr 1	Qtr 2	Qtr 3	Qtr 4
Creditors (2)	13.80	14.80	20.20	17.20
Direct labour (4)	13.80	15.00	16.20	16.20
Variable overhead (5)	8.25	9.75	11 25	10.50
Fixed overhead minus depreciation (6)	14.50	14.50	14.50	14.50
Capital expenditure		20.00		
Dividends	15.00			
Total cash outflow	65.35	74.05	62.15	58.40
Net movement in cash during quarter	−3.35	−4.05	+19.82	+29 60
Cash balance at beginning of quarter	+1.00	−2.35	−6.40	+13.45
Cash balance at end of quarter	−2.35	−6.40	+13.45	+43.05

Notes:

	Qtr 1 £000	Qtr 2 £000	Qtr 3 £000	Qtr 4 £000
(1) *Calculation of receipts from debtors*:				
Opening balance	40			
4 weeks current quarter sales (4/12)	22	26	30	28
8 weeks previous quarter sales (8/12)	–	44	52	60
	62	70	82	88

	Qtr 1 £000	Qtr 2 £000	Qtr 3 £000	Qtr 4 £000
(2) *Calculation of payments to creditors:*				
Materials purchased (20% of sales, see Note 3)	13.2	15.6	18.0	16.8
Opening balance	5.0			
8 weeks current quarter purchase (8/12)	8.8	10.4	12.0	11.2
4 weeks previous quarter purchases (4/12)	–	4.4	5.2	6.0
Stock increase			3.0	
	13.8	14.8	20.2	17.2

(3) Direct materials are 25% of sales for year ending 30 November 1982. For year ending 30 November 1983, the prices of materials are 20% lower. Therefore materials are 20% (80% × 25%) of sales for 1983. It is assumed that materials usage remains unchanged.

(4)	Qtr 1 £000	Qtr 2 £000	Qtr 3 £000	Qtr 4 £000
Existing employees (£12,000 + 15%)	13.8	13.8	13.8	13.8
Additional operations		1.2	2.4	2.4
	13.8	15.0	16.2	16.2

(5) For year ending 30 November 1982, variable overheads are 12½% of sales. Quarterly variable overheads are assumed to be 12½% of quarterly sales for 1983.

(6)	£
Fixed overheads for 1982	70,000
Less depreciation	24,000
	46,000
Add increase for 1983	12,000
Total fixed overheads for 1983	58,000
Quarterly fixed overheads	14,500

Answer to question 13.15

(a) See the section on why we do produce budgets in Chapter 13 for the answer to this question.

(b) (i)

	kg
Normal production: 1,750 kg of product X per week for 4 weeks =	7,000
Overtime working 5 hours × 50 kg × 4 weeks =	1,000
Total production	8,000
Opening stock	6,500
Production	8,000
	14,500
Sales	9,000
Closing stock	5,500

(ii) *Material purchases budget*:

	A kg	B kg	C kg
Closing stock requirements (1)	5,250	3,500	1,750
Production (2)	6,000	4,000	2,000
	11,250	7,500	3,750
Less opening stock	5,000	5,000	1,000
Purchases	£6,250	£2,500	£2,750
Price per kilo	£1	£0.50	£0.75
Cost of purchases	£6,250	£1,250	£2,062.50
Total purchase cost	£9,562.50		

Notes:
(1) A = 7,000/20 × 15; B = 7,000/20 × 10; C = 7,000/20 × 5
(2) A = 8,000/20 × 15; B = 8,000/20 × 10; C = 8,000/20 × 5

(iii) *Production cost budget*:

	£	£
Materials: A (6,000 × £1)	6,000	
B (4,000 × £0.50)	2,000	
C (2,000 × £0.75)	1,500	9,500
Labour (1)		34,000
Production Overhead (2)		20,000
		63,500

Notes:

	£
(1) Normal time 50 × £140 × 4 weeks	28,000
Overtime 50 × 5 hours × £6 × 4 weeks	6,000
	34,000

(2) Overhead absorption rate = £2.50 per hour (£218,750/87,500 hours). Overhead charged to production = 50 × 40 hours × 4 weeks × £2.50 = £20,000.

Answer to question 13.16

(a) (i) *Sales revenue budget*:

	Alpha £	Beta £	Gamma £	Total £
Northern region	180,000	550,000	360,000	1,090,000
Southern region	300,000	770,000	540,000	1,610,000
Total	480,000	1,320,000	900,000	2,700,000

(ii) *Production budget*:

	Alpha £	Beta £	Gamma £	Total £
Opening stock	1,000	1,200	1,500	3,700
Closing stock	1,200	1,000	1,800	
Increase (decrease) in stock	200	(200)	300	
Sales	8,000	12,000	10,000	
Production	8,200	11,800	10,300	30,300

(iii) *Material purchase budget*:

	X £	Y £	Total £
Opening stock	5,000	7,500	
Closing stock	8,000	10,000	
Increase in stock	3,000	2,500	
Alpha 8,200 × 2	16,400	× 3 24,600	
Beta 11,800 × 3	35,400	× 4 47,200	
Gamma 10,300 × 2.5	25,750	× 1.5 15,450	
Total usage	80,550	87,250	
	× £3	× £2	
Cost	241,650	174,500	416,150

(iv) *Labour cost budget*:

	Alpha	Beta	Gamma	Total
Production (units)	8,200	11,800	10,300	30,300

	Department 1 £	Department 2 £	Total £
Alpha	8,200 × 0.75 = 6,150	× 1.5 = 12,300	18,450
Beta	11,800 × 1.25 = 14,750	× 2.0 = 23,600	38,350
Gamma	10,300 × 2.0 = 20,600	× 2.5 = 25,750	46,350
Budgeted labour hours	41,500	61,650	103,150
× Labour rate	£4	£3	
Labour cost	£166,000	£184,950	£350,950

(v) *Overhead absorption rates*:

		Department 2 Machine hours
Alpha	(8.200 × 2)	16,400
Beta	(11,800 × 2)	23,600
Gamma	(10,300 × 3)	30,900
Production machine hours		70,900

	Department 2 machine hour overhead rate	£8	(£567,200/70,900 hrs)
	Department 1 direct labour hour overhead rate	£10	(£415,000/41,500 hrs)

(vi) *Product cost budget:*

	Alpha	Beta	Gamma
	£	£	£
Material X	2 × 3 = 6	3 × 3 = 9	2.5 × 3 = 7.5
Y	3 × 2 = 6	4 × 2 = 8	1.5 × 2 = 3
	12	17	10.5
Labour Department 1	0.75 × 4 = 3	1.25 × 4 = 5	2 × 4 = 8
Department 2	1.5 × 3 = 4.5	2.0 × 3 = 6	2.5 × 3 = 7.5
	7.5	11	15.5
	£	£	£
Production overhead: Department 1	0.75 × £10 = 7.5	1.25 × £10 = 12.5	2 × £10 = 20
Department 2	2.0 × £8 = 16	2.0 × £8 = 16	3 × £8 = 24
	23.5	28.5	44
Production cost	43.0	56.5	70
Administration cost (1)	7.5	11.0	15.5
	50.5	67.5	85.5
Profit	9.5	42.5	4.5
Selling price	60.0	110.0	90.0

Note:

(1)   Administration overhead rate $= \dfrac{\text{Administration overhead}}{\text{Labour Cost}} = \dfrac{£350,950}{£350,950}$

$= £1$ per £1 of D.L.

Answer to question 13.18

(a)   (i)   *Sales budget*:

	Quarter 1	Quarter 2	Quarter 3	Quarter 4	Total
Sales units	40,000	50,000	30,000	45,000	165,000
Unit price (£)	150	150	160	160	
Revenue (£000)	6,000	7,500	4,800	7,200	25,500

(ii)   *Production budget (units):*

Opening stock	9,000	5,000	3,000	4,500	
Production (difference)	36,000	48,000	31,500	44,500	160,000
	45,000	53,000	34,500	49,000	
Closing stock^a	5,000	3,000	4,500	4,000	
Sales	40,000	50,000	30,000	45,000	

Note:
^{a}10% of next quarter's sales.

(iii)   *Material usage budget (units):*

					Total
	(000)	(000)	(000)	(000)	(000)
Component R	144 (36,000 × 4)	192	126	178	640
Component T	108 (36,000 × 3)	144	94.5	133.5	480
Shell S	36 (36,00 × 1)	48	31.5	44.5	160

(iv) *Production cost budget:*

	(000)	(000)	(000)	(000)	Total (000)
Materials:					
Component R	1,152	1,689.60	1,108.80	1,566.40	5,516.80
Component T	540	792.00	519.75	734.25	2,586.00
Shell S	1,080	1,440.00	945.00	1,335.00	4,800.00
	2,772	3,921.60	2,573.55	3,635.65	12,902.80
Labour (at £30 per unit)	1,080	1,440.00	945.00	1,388.40	4,853.40
Variable overhead	360	480.00	315.00	445.00	1,600.00
Fixed overhead[a]	54	72.00	47.25	66.75	240.00
Total production cost	4,266	5,913.60	3,880.80	5,535.80	19,596.20

Note:
[a]Charged out at £1.50 per unit of output (£240,000/160,00 units)

(b) The principal budget factor is the factor which limits the organization's ability to achieve increasing profits. In most organizations the principal budget factor is sales. For a brief discussion of how sales may be forecast see the section on preparation of the sales budget in Chapter 13.

Answer to question 13.21

(a) The answer should describe the benefits arising from the planning, co-ordinating, communicating, motivating, control and evaluation roles of budgets. See the section on why do we produce budgets in Chapter 13 for the answer to this question.

(b) The revised standards (in kg per hundred units) for material B are as follows:

Product 1   2.7   (3.0 × 90%)
2   0.45   (0.5 × 90%)
4   1.8   (2.0 × 90%)

Production equals sales for all products except for product 5 where production equals sales (900,000 units) plus stock increase (30% × 100,000 units).

Material usage budget (kg):

	Product					
	1	2	3	4	5	Total
Material A:						
kg/100 per units	2.5	7.0	1.5	–	5.5	
× production (100 units)	6,000	3,500	18,500	–	9,300	
= usage (kg)	15,000	24,500	27,750	–	51,150	118,400
Material B:						
kg/100 units	2.7	0.45	–	1.8	–	
× production (100 units)	6,000	3,500	–	12,000	–	
= usage (kg)	16,200	1,575	–	21,600	–	39,375

Material purchases budget (kg):

	Material A	Material B
Budgeted usage	118,400	39,375
± Change in stock	1,810	(322.5)
	120,210	39,052.5

(c) *Standard material usage for actual production:*

		kg	
Product	1	14,500	(580,000 × 25 per 1,000 units)
	2	23,100	(330,000 × 70 per 1,000 units)
	3	28,500	(1,900,000 × 15 per 1,000 units)
	5	44,000	(800,000 × 55 per 1,000 units)
		110,100	

Standard material cost for actual production = £264,240 (110,100 × £2.40)

$$
\begin{aligned}
\text{Material price variance} &= (\text{standard price} - \text{actual price}) \times \text{actual quantity} \\
&= (\text{actual quantity} \times \text{standard price}) \\
&\quad - (\text{actual quantity} \times \text{actual price}) \\
&= (116,250 \times £2.40 - £280,160) \\
&= £1,160 \text{ adverse}
\end{aligned}
$$

Journal entries:

	£	£
Dr Material A stores ledger account (AQ × SP)	279,000	
Dr Material price variance account	1,160	
Cr Creditors control account		280,160
Purchase of material A:		
Dr WIP control account (SQ × SF)	264,240	
Cr Material A stores ledger account		264,240

Answer to question 13.22

(a) *Raw materials:*

(Units)	March	April	May	June
Opening stock	100	110	115	110
Add: Purchases	80	80	85	85
	180	190	200	195
Less: Used in production	70	75	90	90
Closing stock	110	115	110	105
(Units) *Finished production:*				
Opening stock	110	100	91	85
Add: Production	70	75	90	90
	180	175	181	175
Less: Sales	80	84	96	94
Closing stock	100	91	85	81

(b) *Sales:*

	March	April	May	June	Total
(at £219 per unit)	£17,520	£18,396	£21,024	£20,586	£77,526
Production cost:					
Raw materials (using FIFO)	3,024 (1)	3,321 (2)	4,050	4,050	14,445
Wages and variable costs	4,550	4,875	5,850	5,850	21,125
	£7,574	£8,196	£9,900	£9,900	£35,570

Debtors:

Closing debtors = May + June sales = £41,610

Creditors:

June purchases 85 units × £45   £3,825

Notes:

(1) 70 units × £4,320/100 units = £3,024.

(2) (30 units × £4,320/100 units) + (45 units × £45) = £3,321.

Closing stocks:

Raw materials 105 units × £45   £4,725

Finished goods 81 units × £110[(1)]   £8,910

Note:

[(1)] Materials (£45) + Labour and Variable Overhead (£65).

It is assumed that stocks are valued on a variable costing basis.

(c) *Cash budget:*

		March £	April £	May £	June £
Balance b/fwd		6,790	4,820	5,545	132,415
Add: Receipts					
Debtors (two months credit)		7,680	10,400	17,520	18,396
Loan		–	–	120,000	–
	(A)	14,470	15,220	143,065	150,811
Payments:					
Creditors (one month's credit)		3,900	3,600	3,600	3,825
			(80 × £45)		
Wages and variable overheads		4,550	4,875	5,850	5,850
Fixed overheads		1,200	1,200	1,200	1,200
Machinery		–	–	–	112,000
Interim dividend		–	–	–	12,500
	(B)	9,650	9,675	10,650	135,375
Balance c/fwd	(A) – (B)	4,820	5,545	132,415	£15,436

(d) *Master budget:*

Budgeted trading and profit and loss account for the four months to 30 June 19X5

	£	£
Sales		77,526
Cost of sales: Opening stock finished goods	10,450	
Add: Production cost	35,570	
	46,020	
Less: Closing stock finished goods	8,910	37,110
		40,416
Less: Expenses		
Fixed overheads (4 × £1,200)	4,800	
Depreciation		
Machinery and equipment	15,733	
Motor vehicles	3,500	
Loan interest (2/12 × $7\frac{1}{2}$% of £120,000)	1,500	25,533
		14,883
Less: Interim dividends		12,500
		2,383
Add: Profit and loss account balance b/fwd		40,840
		£43,223

Budgeted balance sheet as at 30 June 19X5:

Fixed assets	Cost £	Depreciation to date £	Net £
Land and buildings	500,000	–	500,000
Machinery and equipment	236,000	100,233	135,767
Motor vehicles	42,000	19,900	22,100
	778,000	120,133	657,867

Current assets			
Stock of raw materials		4,725	
Stock of finished goods		8,910	
Debtors		41,610	
Cash and bank balances		15,436	
		70,681	
Less: Current liabilities			
Creditors	3,825		
Loan interest owing	1,500	5,325	65,356
			£723,223

Capital employed	£
Ordinary share capital £1 shares (fully paid)	500,000
Share premium	60,000
Profit and loss account	43,223
	603,223
Secured loan ($7\frac{1}{2}\%$)	120,000
	£723,223

Answer to question 13.23

(a)		Product 1	Product 2	Product 3
(i)	Sales	850,000	1,500,000	510,000
(ii)	Stock change	100,000	45,000	(35,000)
(iii)	Units packed	950,000	1,545,000	475,000
(iv)	Rejects [5/95 × (iii)]	50,000	–	25,000
(v)	Units filled	1,000,000	1,545,000	500,000
(vi)	Units filled per hour	125	300	250
(vii)	Units packed per hour	95	100	95
(viii)	DLHs required:			
	Filling [(v)/(vi)]	8,000	5,150	2,000
	Packing [(iii)/(vii)]	10,000	15,450	5,000
	Total DLHs	18,000	20,600	7,000

Total hours required for direct labour personnel = (18,000 + 20,600 + 7,000)/
0.8 = 57,000 hours
Hours per employee per annum = 38 hours × 50 weeks = 1,900 hours
Direct labour personnel required = 30 (57,000 hours/1,900 hours)

(b)   £
Payroll cost: Basic pay (30 × 35 hours × 52 weeks × £4) =   218,400
Overtime (30 × 3 hours × 52 weeks × £5)   =   23,400
                                                          241,800

Direct labour hour rate = £5.30 (£241,800/45,600 DLHs)

(c)   Product 1   Product 2   Product 3
Filling   4.46 p [£5.30/(0.95 × 125)]   1.77 p (£5.30/300)   2.23 p [£5.30/(0.95 × 250)]
Packing   5.58 p (£5.30/95)   5.30 p (£5.30/100)   5.58 p (£5.30/95)

            10.04 p   7.07 p   7.81 p

Control in the organization

Answers to Chapter 14

Question summary

14.1 to 14.3
Various discussion questions relevant to Chapter 14.

14.4 and 14.5
Preparation of cash and flexible budgets.

14.6 to 14.8
Preparation of flexible budgets. Question 14.6 requires the calculation of fixed and variable costs and 14.7 requires the application of a budget formula to determine the flexible budget allowance. Question 14.8 also requires a discussion of the motivation role of budgets.

14.9
Criticisms and redrafting of a monthly performance report.

14.10 to 14.14
Questions relating to flexible budgeting. Question 14.10 also involves the preparation of sales budgets based on limiting factors. Questions 14.11 and 14.12 require comments and explanations of the variances. Question 14.14 requires the preparation of a performance report adopting a flexible budgeting approach.

14.15
Comments on budget preparation and suggestions for improving the performance reports.

14.16
Sales forecasting, removing seasonal variations, flexible budgets and budget preparation.

Answer to question 14.1

(a) See Chapter 14 for the answer to this problem. In particular your answer should stress:

(i) The need for a system of responsibility accounting based on a clear definition of a manager's authority and responsibility.

(ii) The production of performance reports at frequent intervals comparing actual and budget costs for individual expense items. Variances should be analysed according to whether they are controllable or non-controllable by the manager.

(iii) The managers should participate in the setting of budgets and standards.

(iv) The system should ensure that variances are investigated, causes found and remedial action is taken.

(v) An effective cost control system must not be used as a punitive device but should be seen as a system which helps managers to control their costs more effectively.

(b) Possible problems include:

(i) Difficulties in setting standards for non-repetitive work.

(ii) Non-acceptance by budgetees if they view the system as a punitive device to judge their performance.

(iii) Isolating variances where interdependencies exist.

Answer to question 14.2

See Chapter 14 for the answer to this problem. The answer should also include a discussion of the following techniques:

(a) Budgetary control and standard costing (see Chapter 14 for a discussion of standard costing).

(b) Fixed and flexible budgeting.

Answer to question 14.3

See the section on responsibility accounting in Chapter 14 for the answer to this question.

Answer to question 14.4

(a) See Chapter 13 for a description of each of the terms.

(b)

	Nov. £000	Dec. £000	Jan. £000	Feb. £000	Mar. £000
Sales	50	70	60	80	100
Credit sales (80%)	40	56	48	64	80
Cash received:					
1 month lag (60%)		24	33.6	28.8	38.4
2 month lag (30%)			12	16.8	14.4
Cash sales (20%)	10	14	12	16	20
Total cash received			57.6	61.6	72.8

(i) Debtors at 1 January 1988:

November sales	£16,000 (10 − 24)
December sales	£56,000
	£72,000

(ii) Cash budget:

	Jan.	Feb.	Mar.
	£000	£000	£000
Opening balance	20.0	77.6	139.2
Cash received	57.6	61.6	72.8
Closing balance	77.6	139.2	212.0

(iii) See section on cash budgets in Chapter 13 for the answer to this question. In particular the answer should stress the benefits from reviewing the predicted weekly/monthly cash balances and taking appropriate action in advance to ensure that adequate cash is available to meet planned cash commitments.

(c)

Activity level	70%	85%
Direct labour hours	35,000	42,500
	£	£
Indirect labour	35,000	42,500
Consumable materials	17,500	21,250
Semi-variable costs (1): Fixed	5,200	5,200
Variable	11,200	13,600
Fixed costs	30,000	30,000
	98,900	112,550

Note:

	Direct labour hours	Costs
(1) 65% activity	32,500 (65%)	15,600
90% activity	45,000 (90%)	19,600
	12,500	4,000

Variable cost per direct labour hour	£0.32	(£4,000/12,500 DLHs)
Variable cost for 45,000 DLHs	= £14,400	
Fixed cost (balance)	= £5,200	
	£19,600	

Answer to question 14.8

Task 1:

Performance Statement – Month to 31 October 1996:

Number of guest days =	Original budget	9,600
	Flexed budget	11,160

	Flexed budget	Actual	Variance
Controllable expenses	£	£	£
Food (1)	23,436	20,500	2,936F
Cleaning materials (2)	2,232	2,232	0
Heat, light and power (3)	2,790	2,050	740F
Catering staff wages (4)	8,370	8,400	30A
	36,828	33,182	3,646F
Non-controllable expenses			
Rent, rates, insurance and depreciation (5)	1,860	1,860	0

Notes:

(1) £20,160/9,600 × 11,160.
(2) £1,920/9,600 × 11,160.
(3) £2,400/9,600 × 11,160,
(4) 11,160/40 × £30.
(5) Original fixed budget based on 30 days but October is a 31-day month (£1,800/30 × 31).

Task 2:

(a) See the sections on why do we produce budgets (motivation) in Chapter 13 and the role of the management accountant in the management process (motivation) in Chapter 1 for the answer to this question.

(b) Motivating managers ought to result in improved performance. However, besides motivation, improved performance is also dependent on managerial ability, training, education and the existence of a favourable environment. Therefore motivating managers is not guaranteed to lead to improved performance.

(c) The use of a fixed budget is unlikely to encourage managers to become more efficient where budgeted expenses are variable with activity. In the original performance report actual expenditure for 11,160 guest days is compared with budgeted expenditure for 9,600 days. It is misleading to compare actual costs at one level of activity with budgeted costs at another level of activity. Where the actual level of activity is above the budgeted level adverse variances are likely to be reported for variable cost items. Managers will therefore be motivated to reduce activity so that favourable variances will be reported. Therefore it is not surprising that Susan Green has expressed concern that the performance statement does not reflect a valid reflection of her performance. In contrast, most of Brian Hilton's expenses are fixed and costs will not increase when volume increases. A failure to flex the budget will therefore not distort his performance.

   To motivate, challenging budgets should be set and small adverse variances should normally be regarded as a healthy sign and not something to be avoided. If budgets are always achieved with no adverse variances this may indicate that undemanding budgets may have been set which are unlikely to motivate best possible performance. This situation could apply to Brian Hilton who always appears to report favourable variances.

Answer to question 14.9

(a) The report should include the following points:

   (i) Actuals are compared with a fixed budget which results in a comparison of actual and budgeted expenses for different output levels. Flexible budgeting should be adopted for performance reporting.

   (ii) Variances should be analysed into their price and quantity elements since different managers are likely to be accountable for different categories of variances.

   (iii) The report is confusing with both physical volumes and values being presented for each budgeted items. They should be reported separately to avoid confusion.

   (iv) The report should be split into two separate sections   a section for controllable expenses and another for uncontrollable expenses. It is possible that all the expenses are controllable but if this is the case it should be clearly indicated in the report. No controllable fixed costs are included in the report. If such expenses do exist they should be reported separately.

   (v) No indication is given of the output which should have been attained from the actual level of activity.

Revised Monthly Variance Report:

Original budget : Sales volume
                 : Production volume

Actuals   : Sales volume
                 : Production volume

	Flexed budget £	Actuals £	Quantity variance £	Price variance £	Total variance £	Cumulative variances for the year £
Sales (based on original budget)						
Less controllable expenses:						
Direct materials						
Direct labour						
Controllable contribution						
Less controllable fixed costs						
Controllable profit						

(b) Standard costing is most suited to controlling those activities that involve repetitive operations. Standard costing procedures cannot easily be applied to non-manufacturing activities where the operations are of a non-repetitive nature, since there is no basis for observing repetitive operations and consequently standards cannot easily be set.

   Where standards cannot easily be applied budgets are used to control costs. A budget relates to an entire activity or operations where standards can be applied to the units of output and thus provide a basis for the detailed analysis of variances.

A single organization might use standard costing to control the costs relating to manufacturing activities and budgetary control to control the costs of support departments and non-manufacturing activities.

Answer to question 14.11

(a) *Budget statement:*

Overhead	Budget Fixed £	Budget Variable £	Total £	Actual £	Variance Adv. £	Variance Fav. £
Management	30,000	–	30,000	30,000	–	–
Shift premium	–	3,600	3,600	4,000	400	
National Insurance	6,000	7,920	13,920	15,000	1,080	
Inspection	20,000	9,000	29,000	28,000		1,000
Supplies	6,000	6,480	12,480	12,700	220	
Power	–	7,200	7,200	7,800	600	
Light and heat	4,000	–	4,000	4,200	200	
Rates	9,000	–	9,000	9,000	–	
Repairs	8,000	5,400	13,400	15,100	1,700	
Materials handling	10,000	10,800	20,800	21,400	600	
Depreciation	15,000	–	15,000	15,000	–	
Administration	12,000	–	12,000	11,500		500
Idle time	–	–	–	1,600	1,600	
					6,400	1,500
	£120,000	£50,400	£170,400	£175,300	£4,900A	

(b) *National Insurance.* It appears that National Insurance rates have increased. If this assumption is correct then the variance will be beyond the control of management. Note that actual activity is less than budgeted activity. It is therefore unlikely that total wages will have increased because of an increase in the number of labour hours worked. It is possible that wage rates have increased thus increasing the National Insurance payments. (Note that National Insurance payments are a fixed percentage of wages.)

Inspection. It is possible that the standard of inspection has been lowered thus resulting in a saving in costs. If this has not been a policy decision taken by management then the variance should be investigated. Another possibility is that a member of staff has resigned. Consequently. the actual labour cost will be less than the budget.

Repairs and maintenance. This variance may be due to unexpected repairs which were not envisaged when the budget was set. It is unlikely that variances for repairs and maintenance will fluctuate considerably from month to month. It is therefore appropriate to compare budgeted and actual expenditure for several months rather than focus on a single month.

Idle time. No allowance for normal idle time is included in the budget. Consequently, the idle time must be of an abnormal nature. Possible uncontrollable causes include power failures or machine breakdowns. Controllable causes include bottlenecks arising from poor production scheduling or a lack of materials.

(c) (i) Concentrating on variances in excess of a specific figure may not be satisfactory for control purposes. Variances should be investigated only if the investigation is likely to yield benefits in terms of identifying inefficiencies and remedying them. It may be preferable to use statistical tests to establish the probability that the variance is out of control.

(ii) The statement could be improved by analysing the expense items into their controllable and non-controllable elements Where possible, variances should be analysed according to whether they are due to price and quantity changes. The statements should also include non-financial measures such as a comparison of actual hours worked with standard hours produced.

(d) (i) Overhead absorbed = £158,400 (£4.40 × 36,000 hours).

(ii) Overspending = £4,900 (see part (a) of answer).

(iii) Actual production was 4,000 standard hours less than budgeted production and this decline in output has resulted in a failure to recover £12,000 fixed overheads. This under recovery of £12,000 is also known as the volume variance.

Answer to question 14.13

(a) Actual volume exceeds the budgeted volume by $12\frac{1}{2}$% [(720 − 640)/640]. Therefore all of the variable costs are increased by $12\frac{1}{2}$% and the fixed costs remain unchanged in the flexed operating statement reproduced below.

Flexed operating statement based on actual sales volume of 720,000 units:

	Budget £000	Actual £000	Variance £000
Sales	1,024	1,071	47
Cost of sales			
Materials	189	144	45
Labour	270	288	(18)
Overheads (Variable)	36	36	Nil
Labour (Fixed)	100	94	6
	595	562	33
Selling and distribution costs			
Fixed	72	83	(11)
Variable	162	153	9
	234	236	(2)
Administration			
Fixed	184	176	8
Variable	54	54	Nil
	238	230	8
Net profit	(43)	43	86

Possible reasons for variances:
Actual sales volume exceeds budgeted sales volume thus generating revenues in excess of budgets. However, actual selling price was less than budgeted selling price but the overall effect has been favourable in terms of sales revenues.

The favourable material variance may be due to negotiating more favourable prices and/or more efficient usage of the materials.

The adverse labour variance may have arisen because of the purchase of poor quality materials or more overtime being worked to meet the increased sales volume. The decline in the fixed labour cost may have been caused by employees leaving and not being replaced immediately.

The adverse fixed selling and distribution cost variance may be due to an increase in the cost of advertising or extra advertising. The variable element may be due to more efficient distribution methods resulting in a reduction in delivery costs.

The favourable fixed administration cost variance may be due to reduction in rentals of office machinery or office staff leaving and not being replaced immediately.

(b) See the section on flexible budgeting in Chapter 14 for the answer to this question.

(c) The answer should focus on the following points:
   (i) Difficulty in accurately dividing costs into their fixed and variable elements. Past cost and activity information is used to provide an estimate to predict future cost behaviour. Inaccurate estimates will result in the prediction of inaccurate costs.
   (ii) Past information is used to predict future costs. Past trends are normally used to predict price behaviour but what has happened in the past does not always provide a reliable guide for the future.
   (iii) Step fixed costs may occur but it is difficult to predict the exact point where the step increases will occur.
   (iv) Flexible budgeting normally assumes that variable costs are constant per unit but this may be inappropriate if curvilinear cost–volume relationships exist.

Answer to question 14.15

(a) (i) Activity varies from month to month but quarterly budgets are set by dividing total annual expenditure by 4.
   (ii) The budget ought to be analysed by shorter intervals (e.g. monthly) and costs estimated in relation to monthly activity.
   (iii) For control purposes monthly comparisons and cumulative monthly comparisons of planned and actual expenditure to date should be made.
   (iv) The budget holder does not participate in the setting of budgets.
   (v) An incremental budget approach is adopted. A zero-base approach would be more appropriate.
   (vi) The budget should distinguish between controllable and uncontrollable expenditure.

(b) The information which should flow from a comparison of the actual and budgeted expenditure would consist of the variances for the month and year to date analysed into the following categories:

    (i) controllable and uncontrollable items;

    (ii) price and quantity variances with price variance analysed by inflationary and non-inflationary effects;

(c) (i) Flexible budgets should be prepared on a monthly basis. Possible measures of activity are number of patient days or expected laundry weight.

    (ii) The laundry manager should participate in the budgetary process.

    (iii) Costs should be classified into controllable and non-controllable items.

    (iv) Variances should be reported and analysed by price and quantity on a monthly and cumulative basis.

    (v) Comments should be added explaining possible reasons for the variances.

Standard costing and variance analysis

Answers to Chapter 15

Question summary

15.1 to 15.12
Multiple choice questions.

15.13 and 15.14
Calculation of material and labour variances. Question 15.14 requires the calculation of variances and inputs and outputs from incomplete data.

15.15
Calculation of labour, material and sales variances plus a reconciliation of actual and budgeted profit. Part (b) requires accounting entries for a standard costing system for the purchase and issue of materials.

15.16
Calculation of labour and material variances for a hotel.

15,17 and 15.18
Calculation of labour and material variances and reconciliation of standard and actual cost.

15.19 to 15.25
Calculation of overhead variances. Question 15.20 requires the computation of the budgeted inputs and 15.24 also requires the calculation of labour and material variances.

15.26 to 15.28
Reconciliation of standard and actual costs or budgeted and actual profit involving labour, material and overhead variances.

15.29 to 15.34
Calculation of actual inputs working backwards from reported variances given in the question and the calculation of variances from incomplete information.

15.35
Comparison of standard absorption costing and standard marginal costing.

15.36 to 15.39

Accounting entries for a standard costing system. Question 15.36 requires the preparation of the stores ledger account when the price variance is extracted at the time of issue and also at the time of purchase. Questions 15.37 to 15.39 require the calculation of labour, material and overhead variances. A full absorption costing system is operated with Questions 15.37 and 15.39 whereas 15.38 assumes that a variable costing system is in operation.

Question 15.38 also assumes that the company uses an interlocking accounting system.

15.40 and 15.41

Calculation of productivity ratios. Question 15.40 also involves the calculation of labour and material variances.

Answer to question 15.13

(a)   (i)   Flexed budget for month 6.

	Original budget	Flexed budget	Actual costs	Total variances
Units of J	20,000	18,500	18,500	
	£	£	£	£
Direct materials	480,000	444,000	442,650	1,350F
Direct labour	140,000	129,500	129,940	440A
Variable overhead	60,000	55,500	58,800	3,300A
Fixed overhead	100,000	100,000	104,000	4,000A
	780,000	729,000	735,390	6,390A

(ii)

Material price variance = (Standard price − Actual price) Actual quantity
= (AQ × SP) − (AQ × AP)
= (113,500 × £4) − £442,650 Actual cost) = £11,350F

Material usage variance = (Standard quantity − Actual quantity) × Standard price
= (18,500 × 6 = 111,000 − 113,500) × £4 = £10,000A

Wage rate variance = (Standard rate − Actual rate) × Actual hours
= (SR × AH) − (AR × AH)
= (£7 ×17,800) − £129,940 = £5,340A

Labour efficiency variance = (Standard hours − Actual hours) × Standard rate
= (18,500 × 1 hour = 18,500 hours − 17,800) £7
= £4,900F

(b)   See the section on the budget period in Chapter 13 for a description of rolling budgeting (i.e. rolling forecasts).

Answer question 15.14

(a) *Standard product costs (per 100 units):*

	Product 1	Product 2
	£	£
Direct materials	76.44 (98 kg × £0.78)	96.72(33 kg × £2.931)
Direct labour	42.00 (10 hours × £4.20)	40.50 (9 hours × £4.50)
Production overhead	36.00 (10 hours × £3.60)	26.10 (9 hours × £2.90)
	154.44	163.32

(b) (i) Material price variance:
   (Standard price − Actual price) × Actual quantity
   (£0.78   £0.785) × 41,200 = £206A

(ii) Material usage variance:
   (Standard quantity − Actual usage) × Standard price
   [(42,100/100) × 98 − 41,200] × £0.78 = £45F

(iii) Total direct materials variance (£206A + £45F) = £161A

(iv) Wage rate variance:
   (Standard rate − Actual rate) × Actual hours
   (£4.20 − £4.20) × 4,190 = 0

(v) Labour efficiency variance:
   (Standard hours − Actual hours) × Standard rate
   [(42,100/100) × 10 − 4,190] × £4.20 = £84F

(vi) Total overhead variance.
   (Standard cost − Actual cost)
   [(42,100/10) × £3.60 − £14.763] = £393F

(c) Standard cost of material N − Actual cost = Total variance
   Standard cost − £23,828 = £228A
   Standard cost = £23,828 − £228 = £23,600
   Actual production × Standard unit material cost = Standard cost
   Actual production × £96.72/100 = £23,600
   Actual production = 23,600/(£96.72/100) = 24,400 units (vii)
   (Standard quantity − Actual quantity) × Standard price = Material usage variance
   [(24,400/100) × 33 kg − AQ] × £2,931 = £5F
   2,931 AQ = (8.052 × 2,931) − 5
   2,931 AQ = 23,595
   AQ = 8,050 kg (viii)
   Actual price per kg of material N = £23,828/8,050 kg = £2.96 per kg (ix)
   (Standard hours − Actual hours) × Standard rate = Labour efficiency variance
   [(24,400/100) × 9 hours − AH] × £4.50 = £342F
   4.50 AH = (2,196 × 4.50) − 342
   4.50 AH = 9,540
   Actual hours = 2,120 hours (x)
   Actual wages cost = 2,120 hours × £4.55 = £9,646 (xi)
   Standard overhead cost − Actual overhead incurred = Overhead variance
   (2,196 SHP × £2.90) − Overhead incurred = £142A
   Overhead incurred = £6,368 + £142 = £6,510 (xii)

Department Y wage rate variance = (£4.50 − £4.55) × 2,120 hours = 106A (xiii)

Department Y total wages variance = £106A + £342F = £236F (xiv)

Answer to question 15.15

(a) (i) *Actual profit – Period 4:*

	£	£
Sales (450 × £110)		49,500
Materials	10,800	
Wages	18,000	
	28,800	
Less closing stock (50 × £70)	3,500	25,300
Gross profit		24,200
Administration fixed costs		3,000
Profit		£21,200

(ii) Material price =
(Standard price − Actual price) × Actual quantity =
(£10 − £10,800/1,200) × 1,200 = £1,200F

Material usage =
(Standard quantity − Actual quantity) × Standard price =
(500 × 2 − 1,200) × £10 = £2,000A

Wage rate =
(Standard rate − Actual rate) × Actual hours =
(£10 − £18,000/2,000) × 2,000 = £2,000F

Labour efficiency =
(Standard hours − Actual hours) × Standard rate =
(500 × 5 − 1,900) × £10 = £6,000F

Idle time variance = 100 hours × £10   £1,000A

(iii) To reconcile actual and budgeted profits it is necessary to compute the sales margin variances.

Sales margin price =
(Actual margin − Standard margin) × Actual quantity =

$$\left\{ \frac{£49,500}{£450} - £70 - (£100 - £70) \right\} × 450 = £4,500F$$

Sales margin quantity =
(Actual quantity − Budgeted quantity) × Standard margin =
(450 − 500) × £30 = £1,500A

Reconciliation of actual profit and budgeted profit:

	£	£
Budgeted profit (W1)		13,000
Add favourable variances:		
Material price	1,200	
Wage rate	2,000	
Labour efficiency	6,000	
Sales margin price	4,500	13,700
		26,700

Less adverse variances:
Material usage		2,000	
Idle time		1,000	
Sales margin quantity		1,500	
Administration fixed expenses			
(£2,000 − £3,000)		1,000	5,500
Actual profit			21,200

Working:

W1 Budgeted profit: 500 units at £30 budgeted profit margin

	£
	15,000
Less administration expenses	2,000
	13,000

(b) (i) See section on calculation on quantity purchased or quantity used in Chapter 15 for the answer to this problem.

(ii)

	£	£
Dr Stores ledger control account (100 × £1)	100	
Dr Material price variance account	50	
Cr creditors		150

Being purchase of materials:

Dr WIP (60 × £1)	60	
Cr Stores ledger control account		60

It is assumed that there is no material usage variance so that the 60 units issued represent the standard and actual quantity.

Answer to question 15.19

(a)
$$\text{Budgeted fixed overhead rate} = \frac{\text{Fixed overheads (£22,260)}}{\text{Direct labour hours (8,400)}} = \text{£2.65}$$

Standard hours per unit of output = 8,400 hours/1,200 units = 7 hours
Actual production in standard hours = 1,100 × 7 hours = 7,700 hours

Fixed overhead variance = Standard cost for actual production − Actual cost
= 7,700 × £2.65 = £20,405 − £25,536
= £5,131 Adverse

Fixed overhead expenditure variance = Budgeted cost − Actual cost
= £22,260 − £25,536 = £3,276A

Fixed overhead efficiency = (Standard hours − Actual hours) Standard rate
= (7,700 − 7,980) × £2.65
= 742A

Fixed overhead capacity = (Actual hours − Budgeted hours) Standard rate
= (7,980 − 8,400) × £2.65
= £1,113A

Variance summary: £
Fixed overhead expenditure variance = 3,276A
Fixed overhead efficiency variance = 742A
Fixed overhead capacity variance = 1,113A

Total fixed overhead variance 5,131A

(b) See the section on fixed overhead expenditure variance, volume efficiency variance and volume capacity variance in Chapter 15 for the answer to this question.

(c) The purchase of cheaper, poor quality materials may result in a favourable material price variance but may also result in adverse material usage, labour efficiency and overhead efficiency variances.

   Replacing skilled labour with unskilled labour will tend to result in a favourable wage rate variance and also adverse labour efficiency, material usage and overhead efficiency variances.

Answer to question 15.22

(a) The answer should include a description and explanation of the following variances:
   (i)   variable overhead expenditure;
   (ii) variable overhead efficiency;
   (iii) fixed overhead expenditure;
   (iv) fixed overhead efficiency;
   (v)   fixed overhead capacity;
   (vi) fixed overhead volume.
   See Chapter 15 for a description of each of the above variances.

(b) Actual output = 680,000 (completed units) + 25,000 (closing WIP equivalent production) − 21,000 (opening WIP equivalent production)
   = 684,000 units
   Fixed overhead rate = £2 per DLH (£246,000/123,000 DLHs)
   Standard labour hours per unit = 0.2 hours (123,000 DLHs/615,000 units)
   Standard FOAR = £0.40 (0.2 hours × £2 per hour)
   Standard hours produced = 136,800 (684,000 × 0.2 hours)

   Variance analysis
   Expenditure = budgeted cost (£246,000) − actual cost (£259,000)
   = £13,000A
   Volume = [budgeted production (615,000) − actual production (684,000)]
   × FOAR (£0.40)
   = £27,600F
   or
   (123,000 budgeted SHP − 136,800 SHP) × FOAR (£2)
   = £27,600F

   Efficiency = [standard hours produced (136,800) − actual hours (141,000)]
   × FOAR (£2)
   = £8,400A

   Capacity = [actual DLHs (141,000) − budgeted DLHs (123,000)]
   = × FOAR (£2)
   = £36,000F

Answer to question 15.25

(a) Budgeted fixed overhead rate per machine hour = £12 (£5,990,400/499,200 hours)

Budgeted fixed overhead per unit of output = £4 (£5,990,400/1,497,600)

Standard machine hours per unit of output = 0.333 (499,200 hours/1,497,600 units)

Fixed production overhead variance:

$$
\begin{aligned}
\text{Standard cost} - \text{actual cost} &= 123,504 \text{ units} \times £4 \\
&\quad (\text{or } 123,504 \times 0.333 \text{ hrs} \times £12/\text{hr}) \\
&= £494,016 - £492,400 \\
&= £1,616\text{F}
\end{aligned}
$$

Fixed overhead expenditure variance:

$$
\begin{aligned}
\text{Budgeted cost} - \text{actual cost} &= £5,990,400/13 \text{ periods} \\
&= £460,800 - £492,400 \\
&= £31,600\text{A}
\end{aligned}
$$

Fixed overhead volume variance:

$$
\begin{aligned}
(\text{Actual production} &- \text{budgeted production}) \times \text{standard rate} \\
&= (123,504 \text{ units} - 1,497,600 \text{ units}/13) \times £4 \text{ hr} \\
&= £33,216\text{F}
\end{aligned}
$$

Alternatively production can be measured in standard hours:
$[(123,504 \text{ units} \times 0.333 \text{ hrs}) - 38,400 \text{ hrs}] \times £12/\text{hr} = £33,216\text{F}$

Capacity variance:

$$
\begin{aligned}
(\text{Actual hours} &- \text{budgeted hours}) \times \text{standard rate} \\
&= (39,840 \text{ hrs} - 499,200 \text{ hrs}/13) \times £12 \text{ hr} \\
&= £17,280\text{F}
\end{aligned}
$$

Efficiency variance:

$$
\begin{aligned}
(\text{Standard hours} &- \text{actual hours}) \times \text{standard rate} \\
&= (41,168 \text{ hrs} - 39,840 \text{ hrs}) \times £12 \text{ hr} \\
&= £15,936\text{F}
\end{aligned}
$$

For an explanation of each of the above variances you should refer to Chapter 15.

(b) The volume capacity and efficiency variances provide useful information in physical terms as to why actual production differed from budgeted production. The budgeted hours of input were 38,400 (499,200/13) but 39,840 machine hours were actually utilized during the period. If these hours are utilized at their prescribed level of efficiency then they will have resulted in an additional 1,440 hours of output (or 4,320 units of output). The volume efficiency variance indicates that for an actual input of 39,840 hours an output of 41,168 standard hours was obtained. Thus, efficient machine utilization resulted in an additional 1,328 standard hours of output (or 3,984 units of output). Assigning monetary values to these variances is questionable because fixed overheads represent sunk costs.

(c)   The two major events that affected the capacity variance could have been reported separately and a residual capacity variance reported:

	£
Impact of flood (480 hours × £12)	5,760A
Impact of additional shift (1,920 hours × £12)	23,040F
	17,280F
Residual capacity variance	Nil
Total capacity variance	17,280F

Answer to question 15.28

(a)   *Standard product specification:*

Product J:

	£	£
Selling price (120,000/100 units)		1,200
Direct material: R	300	
S	270	
	570	
Direct labour	165	
Prime cost	735	
Fixed production overhead £252,000/1,200)	210	
Total production cost		945
Profit		255

(b)   Material price variance = (standard price − actual price) × actual issues[a]
    Material R: (£30 − £35,000/1,100) × 1,025 kg = £1,866A
    Material S: (£45 − £15,180/345) × 580 kg = £580F

Material usage variance = (standard quantity − actual quantity) × standard rate
    Material R: [(100 units × 10 kg) − 1,025 kg] × £30 = £750A
    Material S: [(100 units × 6 kg) − 580 kg] × £45 = £900F

Wage rate = (standard rate − actual rate) × actual hours
        = (SR × AH) − (AR × AH)
        = (£5.50 × 3,300) − £17,325 = £825F

Labour efficiency variance = (standard hours − actual hours)
                × standard rate
            = [(100 × 30 hrs) − 3,300 hrs] × £5.50
            = £1,650A

Fixed overhead expenditure variances = budgeted cost − actual cost
$$= £252,000/12 − £22,000$$
$$= £1,000A$$

Volume efficiency variance = (standard hours − actual hours)
× standard rate
$$= (3,000 \text{ hrs} − 3,300 \text{ hrs}) × £210/30 \text{ hrs}$$
$$= £2,100A$$

Volume capacity variance = (actual hours − budgeted hours) × standard rate
$$= (3,300 \text{ hrs} − 3,000 \text{ hrs}) × £7$$
$$= £2,100F$$

Note:
[a]Actual issues = purchases + opening stock − closing stock

(c)

	£	£	£
Budgeted gross profit (100 × £255)			25,500
Operating variances:	F	A	
Material price: R		1,866	
S	580		
Material usage: R		750	
S	900		
Direct labour:			
Wage rate	825		
Efficiency		1,650	
Fixed overheads:			
Expenditure		1,000	
Volume efficiency		2,100	
Volume capacity	2,100		
	4,405	7,366	2,961(A)
Actual gross profit			22,539

(d) See possible causes of wage rate and labour efficiency variances in Chapter 15 for the answer to this question.

Answer to question 15.30

(a) (i) Sales margin (profit) volume variance:
(Actual volume − Budgeted volume) × Standard margin (£3) = £5,250 Adverse
(Actual volume × Standard margin) − (Budgeted volume × Standard margin) = £5,250A
(Actual volume × Standard margin) − £30,000 = −£5,250
(Actual volume × Standard margin) = £24,750
Actual volume = £24,750/£3 = 8,250 units

(ii) Labour efficiency variance:
(Standard hours − Actual hours) × Standard rate = £4,000 Adverse
(Standard hours × Standard rate) − (Actual hours × Standard rate) =
−£4,000
(8,250 units × 4 hours = 33,000 × £4) − (Actual hours × £4) =
−£4,000
£132,000 − (Actual hours × £4) = −£4,000
Actual hours × £4 = £136,000
Actual hours = £136,000/£4 = 34,000 hours

(iii) Material usage variance:
(Standard quantity − Actual quantity) × Standard rate = £400F
(Standard quantity × Standard rate) − (Actual quantity × Standard
rate) = £400
(8,250 × 5 litres = 41,250 litres × £0.20) − (Actual quantity × £0.20)
= £400
£8,250 − (Actual quantity × £0.20 = £400
Actual quantity × £0.20 = £7,850
Actual quantity used = 39,250 litres
Actual quantity purchased = 39,250 − stock decrease (800) = 38,450
litres

(iv) Total variable overhead variance:
Standard variable overhead cost − Actual cost = £500 Adverse
(8,250 × £6 = £49,500) − Actual cost = −£500
Actual cost = £50,000

(v) Fixed overhead expenditure variance:
Budgeted cost − Actual cost = £500 Favourable
10,000 units × £14 = £140,000 − Actual cost = £500
Actual cost = £139,500

Note that budgeted output = $\dfrac{\text{Budgeted profit (£30,000)}}{\text{Standard profit margin (£3)}}$

(b) The answer should draw attention to the fact that standard costing is most
suited to an organization whose activities consist of a series of common or
repetitive operations. Standard costing procedures cannot easily be applied
to non-manufacturing activities where the operations are of a non-repetitive nature, since there is no basis for observing repetitive operations and
consequently standards cannot be set.

In those non-manufacturing organizations where routine operations do
not exist, standard costing cannot easily be applied. Instead, budgetary control is used to control costs. A budget relates to an entire activity or operation whereas standards can be applied to the units of output and thus provide a basis for the detailed analysis of variances. Therefore budgeting
focuses on controlling costs at the aggregate level and does not analyse the
difference between actual and budgeted expenditure by price and quantity
variances.

Answer to question 15.32

(a) *Statement of total standard costs for product EM:*

	Actual cost £	Total variance £	Standard cost £
Direct material: E	6,270	270A	6,000
M	650	50A	600
Direct labour	23,200	2,200A	21,000
Variable overhead	6,720	720A	6,000
Fixed overhead	27,000	3,000F	30,000

(b) *Standard product cost:*

	£
Direct material E (1 metre at £10 per metre)	10.00^a
Direct material M (0.333 metres at £3)	1.00^b
Direct labour (5 hours at £7)	35.00^c
Variable overhead (5 hours at £2)	10.00^d
Fixed overhead (5 hours at £10)	50.00^e
	106.00

Notes:
^{a}Standard direct material cost per unit = £6,000/600 units = £10
Actual quantity × standard price = £6,600 (£6,270 + £330)
Standard price per metre = £10 (£6,600/660 metres)
Standard quantity = 1 metre (£10 standard cost/£10 per metre standard price)
^{b}Standard direct material cost per unit = £1 (£600/600 units)
Actual quantity × standard price = £600 (£650 − £50)
Standard price = £3 (£600/200 metres)
Standard quantity = 0.333 metres (£1/£3 metres)
^{c}Standard direct labour cost per unit = £35 (£21,000/600 units)
Actual hours × standard price = £22,400 (£23,200 − £800)
Standard rate = £7 (£22,400/3,200 hours)
Standard quantity = 5 hours (£35/£7 per hour)
^{d}Standard variable overhead rate per unit = £10 (£6,000/600 units)
Standard hours calculated in note c = 5 hours
Standard rate = £2 (£10/5 hours)
^{e}Standard fixed overhead rate per unit = £50 (£30,000/600 units)
Standard hours calculated in note c = 5 hours
Standard fixed overhead rate = £10 (£50/5 hours)

(c) Actual fixed overheads + expenditure variance = budgeted fixed overheads
Budgeted fixed overheads = £27,000 + £500 = £27,500
Budgeted production = budgeted fixed overheads/standard cost
$$= £27,500/£50$$
$$= 550 \text{ units}$$

(d) See the section on establishing cost standards in Chapter 15 for the answer to this question.

Answer to question 15.34

(a) (i)   Budgeted fixed overhead = fixed overhead incurred (£150,000)
$$- \text{ expenditure variance (£6,000)}$$
$$= £144,000$$
Budgeted output = budgeted fixed overhead (£144,000)/standard
$$\text{product overhead cost (£36)}$$
$$= 4,000 \text{ units}$$

(ii)   Price variance = (SP − AP) × actual purchases
£8,000F = (£2.50 − £2.45) × actual purchases
Actual purchases = £8,000/£0.05 = 160,000 litres

(iii)   Usage variance = (standard usage − actual usage) × standard price
$$\text{(£6,000A)}$$
$$= \text{(excess usage)} \times £2.50$$
Excess usage = £6,000/£2.50 = 2,400 litres

(iv)   Standard labour cost = actual cost (£121,500) − total adverse labour
$$\text{variance (£900)}$$
$$= £120,600$$
Actual output = standard labour cost (£120,600)/standard product labour
$$\text{cost (£30)}$$
$$= 4,020 \text{ units}$$

(v)   Wage rate variance = (standard rate − actual rate) × actual hours
£4,500A = (actual hours × standard rate) − actual wages
$$= \text{(actual hours} \times £5) - £21,500$$
AH × £5 = £117,000
AH = £117,000/£5 = 23,400 hours

(vi)   Average wage rate per hour = $\dfrac{\text{actual wages (£121,500)}}{\text{actual hours (23,400)}}$ = £5.19 per hour

(b) Managers at the operational level may have little influence over the monetary values of reported variances. Only materials and variable overheads are likely to vary in the short term with the volume. Direct labour and fixed overheads are fixed sunk costs in the short term, and it is doubtful whether attaching monetary values to these variances provides any useful information for cost control. Indeed, there is a danger that the monetary values of these variances may only serve to confuse operating personnel. A more meaningful indication to shop floor personnel of deviations from the standard might be achieved by focusing on the following:
  (i)   scrap as a percentage of material input;
  (ii)   non-value-added time as a percentage of production hours;
  (iii)   productivity ratios outlined in Chapter 15 (see the section on performance reports);
  (iv)   daily production quantities;
  (v)   percentage of units rejected relative to good units.
For a more detailed discussion of non-financial measures see the section on non-financial measures in Chapter 14.

Answer to question 15.38

(a) *Calculation of variances:*

Material price $= (SP - AP) AQ = (AQ \times SP) - (AQ \times AP)$
$= (34,900 \times £7) - £245,900$
$= £1,600A$

Material usage $= (SQ - AQ) \times SP$
$= [(230,000 \text{ units}/100 \times 15 \text{ kg}) - 34,300] \times £7$
$= £1,400F$

Wage rate $= (SR - AR) AH = (AH \times SR) - (AH \times AR)$
$= (22,900 \times £6) - £138,545$
$= £1,145A$

Labour efficiency $= (SH - AH) \times SR$
$- [(228,000/100 \times 10) - 22,900] \times £6$
$= £600A$

Variable overhead efficiency $= (SH - AH) \times SR$
$= [(228,000/100 \times 10) - 22,900] \times £5$
$= £500A$

Variable overhead expenditure $= (AH \times SR) - \text{actual cost}$
$= (22,900 \times £5) - £113,800$
$= £700F$

Note that actual production for the period is calculated as follows:

	Materials	Labour and overheads
Transferred to finished goods stock	226,000 units	226,000 units
WIP equivalent production	4,000 units	2,000 units
	230,000 units	228,000 units

Raw materials

	£		£
Opening balance[c]	113,400		
Financial ledger control		Work in progress	
(AQ × SF)	244,300	(SQ × SF)	241,500
Material usage variance	1,400	Closing balance	117,600
	359,100		359,100

Wages

	£		£
Financial ledger control	138,545	Labour efficiency variance	600
		Labour rate variance	1,145
		Work in progress	
		(SQ × SP)	136,800
	138,545		138,545

Variable production overheads

	£		£
Financial ledger control	113,800	Work in progress (SQ × SP)	114,000
Variable overhead expenditure variance	700	Variable overhead efficiency variance	500
	114,500		114,500

Fixed production overheads

	£		£
Financial ledger control	196,800	Profit and loss	196,800

Work in progress

	£		£
Raw materials (SQ × SP)	241,500	Finished goods[a]	485,900
Wages (SQ χ SP)	136,800		
Variable production overhead	114,000	Closing balance[b]	6,400
	492,300		492,300

Finished goods

	£		£
Opening balance[c]	597,700	Profit and loss[a]	468,700
Work in progress[a]	485,900	Closing balance[b]	614,900
	1,083,600		1,083,600

Variances

	£		£
Financial ledger control (material price)	1,600	Raw materials (materials usage)	1,400
Wages (labour rate)	1,145	Variable production	
Wages (labour efficiency)	600	overheads (variable	
Variable overhead (variable		production overhead	
production overhead		expenditure)	700
efficiency)	500	Profit and loss	1,745
	3,845		3,845

Profit and loss

	£
Finished goods	468,700
Fixed product overhead	196,800
Variances	1,745

Financial ledger control

	£
Opening balance	711,100
Raw materials	244,300
Variance a/c (raw materials)	1,600
Wages	138,545
Variable overhead	113,800
Fixed overhead	196,800

	£
[a]Completed units transferred:	
To finished goods, 226,000 units at £2.15/unit	485,900
From finished goods, 218,000 units at £2.15/unit	468,700
[b]Closing stocks:	
Raw materials, 16,800 kg at £7/kg	117,600
Work in progress:	
Raw materials, 4,000 units at £1.05 unit	4,200
Labour and variable overhead, 2,000	
equivalent units at £1.10/unit	2,200
	6,400
Finished goods, 286,000 units at £2.15/unit	614,900
[c]Opening stocks:	
Raw materials, 16,200 kg at £7/kg	113,400
Finished goods, 278,000 units at £2.15/unit	597,700

(b) See the section on types of cost standards in Chapter 15 for the answer to this question.

Answer to question 15.39

Workings:

Parts (a) and (b) require a detailed analysis of the variances. The variance calculations are as follows.

	£
Material price: (standard price − actual price) × actual quantity purchased	
Plaster of paris [£8 − (£43,200/5,400)] × 5400	0
Paint [£30 − (£5,800/173)] × 173	610A
Material usage: (standard quantity − actual quantity[a]) × standard price	
Plaster of paris (286[b] × 20 − 5,420) × £8	2,400F
Paint (286 × ½ − 143) × £30	0
Wage rate: (standard rate − actual rate) × actual hours	
(£10 − £11) × 730	730A
Labour efficiency: (standard hours − actual hours) × standard rate	
(286 × 2.5 − 730) × £10	150A
Fixed overhead expenditure (budgeted fixed overheads − actual fixed overheads)	
(300 × £100 − £34,120)	4,120A
Volume efficiency: (standard hours − actual hours) × fixed overhead rate[c]	
(715 − 730) × £40	600A
Volume capacity: (actual hours − budgeted hours) × fixed overhead rate[c]	
(730 − 300 × 2.5) × £40	800A
Sales margin price: (actual selling price − budgeted selling price) × actual sales volume	
(£380 − £380) × 284	0
Sales margin volume: (actual sales quantity[d] − budgeted sales quantity) × standard margin	
(284 − 300) × £80	1,280A

(a) *Stores ledger control account (plaster of paris)*

	(kg)	£		(kg)	£
Balance b/f	2,800	22,400	WIP (SQ × SP)	5,720	45,760
Creditors	5,400	43,200	Balance c/f		
Material usage			(closing stock)	2,780	22,240
variance	300	2,400			
	8,500	68,000		8,500	68,000

Stores ledger control account (paint)

	litres	£		litres	£
Balance c/f	140	4,200	WIP a/c (SQ × SP)	143	4,290
Creditors	173	5,190	Balance c/f		
			(closing stock)	170	5,100
	313	9,390		313	9,390

WIP account

	£		£
Stores ledger control account:		Finished goods stock a/c	85,800
Plaster	45,760		
Paint	4,290		
Wages control account			
(SQ × SP)	7,150		
Fixed overhead account	28,600		
	85,800		85,800

Finished goods stock account

	£		£
Opening balance		Cost of sales (284 × £300)	85,200
(9 × £300)	2,700		
WIP a/c	85,800	Closing stock c/f	3,300
	88,500		88,500

The entries in the creditors, wages and fixed overhead control accounts are shown below:

Creditors

	£
Stores ledger (plaster)	43,200
Stores ledger (paint)	5,190
Material price variance a/c	610

Wages control

	£		£
Wages accrued a/c	8,030	WIP	7,150
		Wage rate variance a/c	730
		Labour efficiency variance a/c	150
	8,030		8,030

Fixed overhead control

	£		£
Expense creditors	34,120	Overhead expenditure variance	4,120
		Volume efficiency	600
		Volume capacity	800
		WIP a/c	28,600
	34,120		34,120

(b) It is assumed that (ii) refers to a statement showing standard profit on actual sales and (iii) refers to a statement showing actual profit.

(i) *Budget trading statement:*

	£	£
Sales revenue (300 × £380)[d]		114,000
Cost of sales: Materials – plaster (300 × £160)	48,000	
– paint (300 × £15)	4,500	
Direct wages (300 × £25)	7,500	
Fixed production overheads (300 × £100)	30,000	
	90,000	
Budgeted profit		24,000

(ii) *Standard cost trading statement:*

	£
Actual sales (284 × £380)	107,920
Standard cost of sales (284 × £300)	85,200
Standard profit on actual sales	22,720

(iii) *Financial trading statement:*

	£	£
Actual sales		107,920
Opening stock[e] (£22,400 + £4,200 + £2,700)	29,300	
Materials (£43,200 + £5,800)	49,000	
Labour	8,030	
Fixed overhead	34,120	
	20,450	
Less closing stock[e] (£22,240 + £5,100 + £3,300)	30,640	89,810
Actual profit		18,110

(iv) *Reconciliation:*

	£
Budgeted profit (i)	24,000
Less sales margin volume variance	1,280
Standard profit on actual sales (ii)	22,720

Cost variances:

	Favourable £	Adverse £	
Paint price		610	
Plaster usage	2,400		
Wage rate		730	
Labour efficiency		150	
Fixed overhead expenditure		4,120	
Volume efficiency		600	
Volume capacity		800	
	2,400	7,010	4,610A
Actual profit (iii)			18,110

Notes:

[a]Note that actual material usage is calculated as follows:

$$\text{opening stock} + \text{purchases} - \text{closing stock}$$

[b]Throughout the answer, actual production and sales are expressed in 100 sets.

[c]The fixed overhead rate is expressed as a rate per standard hour (i.e. 1 hour $\times$ £10 $\times$ 400%).

[d]Note that budgeted production and sales are expressed in 100 sets.

[e]Note that opening and closing stocks are valued at standard cost. The variances are written off as period costs.

Answer to question 15.41

(a) (i)

$$\text{Production volume ratio} = \frac{\text{Standard hours of actual output}}{\text{Budgeted hours of output}} \times 100$$

$$= \frac{(400 \times 5) + (300 \times 2.5) + (140 \times 1)}{(400 \times 5) + (400 \times 2.5) + (100 \times 1)} \times 100 = 93.2\%$$

$$\text{Production efficiency ratio} = \frac{\text{Standard hours of ouput}}{\text{Actual hours worked}} \times 100$$

$$= \frac{(400 \times 5) + (300 \times 2.5) + (140 \times 1)}{2,800 \text{ hrs}} \times 100 = 103.2\%$$

(ii) The production volume ratio shows the relationship between the actual output and budgeted output (both measured in standard hours). Therefore the ratio shows the extent to which the budgeted output was met. The fixed overhead volume variance represents the monetary measure equivalent of the production volume ratio.

The production efficiency ratio represents a labour efficiency measure. During the period 2,890 hours of output were produced but only 2,800 hours were used thus resulting in an efficieny level in excess of 100%. The monetary equivalent variances of this ratio are the labour efficiency, volume efficiency and variable overhead efficiency variances.

(b) Practical capacity is the level of capacity at which a department can normally be expected to operate. It includes an allowance for unavoidable losses in capacity arising from such factors as planned machine maintenance and set-ups.

Budgeted capacity represents the capacity level which is planned to meet the budgeted output for the period. It is based on the budgeted level of efficiency for the period.

Full capacity represents the level of output that could be achieved without any losses or inefficiencies occurring.

Planning and control of stock levels

Answers to Chapter 16

Question summary

For additional questions relating to the calculation of the EOQ and maximum, minimum and reorder levels see Questions 3.10 and 3.12 in Chapter 3.

16.1 and 16.2
Discussion questions relevant to Chapter 16.

16.3 to 16.7
Calculation of EOQ when the purchase cost is constant per unit.

16.8 and 16.10
Calculation of EOQ when the purchase cost per unit varies with the number of units purchased. Both questions require a schedule of costs for different output levels.

16.9
Make-or-buy decision incorporating ordering and holding costs.

Answer to question 16.1

(a) See the section on control of stocks through classification in Chapter 16.

(b) See the section on determining when to place the order in Chapter 16.

(c) See the section on determining the economic order quantity in Chapter 16.

Answer to question 16.3

$EOQ = \sqrt{2DO/H}$
Demand (D) = 90,800 units
Ordering cost (O) = £5,910/30 $\times$ 1.02 = £200.94 per order
Holding cost (H) = £20 per unit $\times$ 15% = £3 per unit

$$EOQ = \sqrt{\frac{2 \times 200.94 \times 90,800}{3}} = 3,488 \text{ units (349 boxes)}$$

Orders per year = $\dfrac{9,080 \text{ boxes annual demand}}{349 \text{ boxes per order}}$ = 26 orders

Order frequency = Every 2 weeks (52 weeks/26 orders per year)

Answer to question 16.7

(a) $EOQ = \sqrt{\dfrac{2DO}{H}}$

where D = total demand for period = 12,500 (3,125 × 4)
     O = ordering cost per batch = £10
     H = holding cost per unit in stock for one year = £1

$$\therefore EOQ = \sqrt{\frac{(2 \times 12,500 \times 10)}{1}} = 500$$

Annual ordering cost = Number of orders × £10

$$= \frac{12,500}{500} \times £10 = £250$$

Annual cost of holding stock = Average stock × £1

$$= \frac{500}{2} \times £1 = £250$$

Therefore minimum annual cost = £250 + £250 = £500

(b)   *Quarterly sales of 781 units:*

Total demand for period = 3,124 (781 × 4)

$$\therefore EOQ = \sqrt{\frac{(2 \times 3,124 \times 10)}{1}} = 250$$

Quarterly sales of 6,250 units:

Total demand for period = 25,000 (6,250 × 4)

$$\therefore EOQ = \sqrt{\frac{(2 \times 25,000 \times 10)}{1}} = 707$$

The EOQ formula shows that the optimal batch size varies in proportion to the square root of total demand (sales volume). Therefore when quarterly sales are 781 units, sales volume changes by a factor of $\frac{1}{4}$ compared with (i). Consequently, the optimal batch size changes by a factor of $\frac{1}{2}$ ($\frac{1}{2} = \sqrt{\frac{1}{4}}$).

When quarterly sales are 6,250 units, sales volume increases by a factor of 2. Therefore, the optimal batch size increases by a factor of $\sqrt{2}$ (= 1,414 approximately).

(c) For an explanation of the economic size $\sqrt{2DO/H}$, see section on determining the economic order quantity (formula method) in Chapter 16.

Answer to question 16.8

Evaluation of optimum order size:

Size of order	No. of orders	Annual purchase cost (W1)		Storage cost	Admin. cost	Total cost
		£		£	£	£
2,400	1	1,728	(£0.72)	300	5	2,033
1,200	2	1,728	(£0.72)	150	10	1,888
600	4	1,824	(£0.76)	75	20	1,919
200	12	1,920	(£0.80)	25	60	2,005
100	24	1,920	(£0.80)	12.50	120	2,052.50

It is recommended that two orders are placed per year for 1,200 units.

		£
Calculation of costs: 2(1,200 × 80p − 10%)	=	1,728
Add: Storage, average quantity held 600 × 25p	=	150
Add: Two orders placed per annum × £5	=	10
		£1,888

Working:

W1 Annual demand of 2,400 units × unit purchase cost.